Grammar and Punctuation

Grammar 5 Teacher's Guide

Carol Matchett

Schofield & Sims

Free downloads available from the Schofield & Sims website

A selection of free downloads is available from the Schofield & Sims website (www.schofieldandsims.co.uk/free-downloads). These may be used to further enhance the effectiveness of the programme. The downloads add to the range of print materials supplied in the teacher's guides. They include the following items:

- a **Curriculum coverage chart**
- an enlarged **Focus text** for each lesson
- a **Dictation assessment sheet**
- a **Pupil target reminder**
- a **Learning pathways class chart** for each year group
- a **Final test analysis class chart** for each year group.

Published by **Schofield & Sims Ltd**, Dogley Mill, Fenay Bridge, Huddersfield HD8 0NQ, UK
Telephone 01484 607080
www.schofieldandsims.co.uk

This edition copyright © Schofield & Sims Ltd, 2017
First published in 2017

Author: **Carol Matchett**
Carol Matchett has asserted her moral rights under the Copyright, Designs and Patents Act, 1988, to be identified as the author of this work.

British Library Cataloguing in Publication Data
A catalogue record for this book is available from the British Library.

Design by **Oxford Designers & Illustrators Ltd**

Printed in the UK by **Page Bros (Norwich) Ltd**

ISBN 978 07217 1399 1

Contents

Introduction

Schofield & Sims Grammar and Punctuation is a structured whole-school scheme for teaching grammar and punctuation while also building on vocabulary, reading and writing skills. It can be used alongside the **Schofield & Sims Spelling** series for complete Spelling, Punctuation and Grammar [SPaG] coverage.

Grammar and Punctuation is designed to progressively develop knowledge and understanding of grammatical concepts through six teacher's guides and six pupil books containing a carefully structured sequence of lessons. The teacher's guides provide you, the teacher or adult helper, with notes and activities to support the teaching of these lessons, annotated answers to the pupil book questions, and a variety of assessment resources for tracking progress.

Supporting a mastery approach, the focus of this programme is on rich practice, deep and secure understanding and fluency in application. Pupils not only learn the terminology and correct usage of grammar and punctuation, but they also build up the skills, knowledge and confidence to apply them in their own independent writing. All pupils are encouraged to move at the same pace through the lessons and are given the same opportunity to fully understand the concept being taught. A wealth of practice questions, writing tasks, activity ideas and resources are provided to support the wider application of the grammar and punctuation that has been learnt in each lesson and to help pupils to truly master the art of writing.

The programme is designed primarily for pupils in Years 1 to 6, and the concepts and terminology that are introduced are in line with the National Curriculum for English. However, understanding of grammar and punctuation is cumulative, so grammatical terms and concepts introduced in one book are revisited and developed further in subsequent books to reinforce the pupils' understanding. In particular, concepts and areas of learning introduced towards the end of one book are revisited and embedded in the next book to further ensure consolidation and continuity.

There are 30 corresponding lessons in **Grammar 5** and its related **Teacher's Guide**, ten for each term. These lessons follow the statutory requirements for Year 5 'Vocabulary, grammar and punctuation' in the National Curriculum for English including Appendix 2, while also promoting and supporting other aspects of the English curriculum. A curriculum coverage chart is available to download from the Schofield & Sims website. An extended glossary can also be found at the back of this teacher's guide [pages 91–96], with a full list of all the terminology relevant to the Year 5 curriculum, along with clear explanations, examples and lesson references.

IMPLEMENTING THE TEACHING MODEL

The **Grammar 5 Teacher's Guide** supports explicit teaching of grammar and punctuation within the wider teaching of reading, writing and speaking. It is based around focused teaching sessions, using the following pedagogical model:

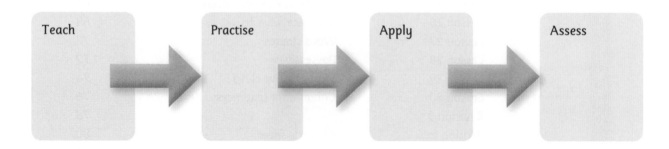

Teach → Practise → Apply → Assess

USING THE TEACHING NOTES

This teacher's guide supports an approach to teaching grammar and punctuation that is systematic, thorough and direct. The teacher's guide provides you with detailed **Teaching notes** for each lesson. A sample page is included below to show the structure of a typical lesson.

Lesson 1 Fronted adverbials: words and phrases

The learning objective of the lesson.

Focus using fronted adverbials [words and phrases] to add detail and for effect

Terminology that the pupils will encounter in the lesson.

Key terms adverbial, adverb, phrase, comma

Focus text Usually, Tyler hated getting up in the morning.
In a faraway land, on a distant hillside, beside a trickling stream, there stood a cottage.
Gradually, the green smoke cleared.
Jane was extremely worried about her son.

A short focus text for use at the start of the lesson.

TEACH

Show the focus text. Explain that these are the opening sentences for four stories. Read and discuss each sentence [e.g. how it draws the reader into the story]. Ask: What makes it intriguing or effective?

Identify and underline the main clause in each sentence [Tyler hated getting up; there stood a cottage; the green smoke cleared; Jane was extremely worried]. Ask the pupils to name the other parts of the sentences [e.g. they are adverbials – adverbs and phrases that tell us more about the event in the main clause].

Discuss what details these adverbials add to the sentences [e.g. details about time – *when* Tyler hated getting up; place – *where* the cottage stood; manner – *how* the smoke cleared; cause – *why* Jane was worried]. Explain that an adverb can also be used to strengthen an adjective [e.g. extremely worried].

Point out that adverbials are often deliberately placed at the start of a sentence, to vary sentence openings or for effect. Discuss the three instances of this in the focus text: how in the first sentence, 'usually' suggests today might be different; how the three fronted adverbials in the second sentence slowly focus in on a place; and how 'gradually' in the third sentence builds tension and suspense.

Invite the pupils to orally compose or write some more opening sentences for stories, using a sentence from the focus text as a model [e.g. In a field, beneath a tree, in a hole in the ground, there lived a …]. Remind them that commas are used after fronted adverbials. When more than one adverbial is added to the start of a sentence, the 'list' of adverbials is separated using commas.

Detailed lesson notes offering guidance on how to teach a specific grammatical feature or concept.

EXTEND Discuss the use of adverbs with adverbials [e.g. only in the morning; really slowly].

Extension of the lesson focus for pupils who want to explore further.

PRACTISE

Pupil book page 4

APPLY

- In stories, the pupils use fronted adverbials to show character [e.g. Enthusiastically, …; Shyly, …] or to emphasise feelings [e.g. Confidently, …; Nervously, …; Patiently, …].
- Encourage the use of fronted adverbials to add a touch of drama or surprise [e.g. To his amazement …].
- The pupils use fronted adverbials in instructions or information texts to add detail or for variety [e.g. With a pencil, carefully draw …; Throughout Britain, …; During the colder winter months, …].

Reference to the relevant pupil book page, which contains practice activities to develop understanding.

ASSESS

Dictation: With a heavy heart, he entered the tunnel. Cautiously, he groped his way through the twisting maze. In the distance, there was the roar of a monster.
Say: Underline all the fronted adverbials.
Check: There is a comma after each fronted adverbial.

10

A dictation activity to assess learning.

Ideas and activities for applying the concept in speech and independent writing.

TEACH

Each lesson begins with an introductory panel featuring the following information:

- **Focus** – The focus of the lesson is clearly stated.
- **Key terms** – The key terminology to be used in the teaching session is listed. Any new terminology that the pupils will come across for the first time in that lesson is highlighted in bold.
- **Focus text** – A short focus text is provided that has been designed for use at the start of the lesson. It is intended that the focus text is written or projected on to a whiteboard to be shared with the pupils. The focus texts cover a range of genres of writing and help to provide a context for the learning that allows the pupils to appreciate the purpose or effect of the target grammar or punctuation feature. All the focus texts are available to download from the Schofield & Sims website.

Clear guidance is given on how to use the **Focus text** at the start of the lesson to 'focus in' on the particular grammar or punctuation feature that you are teaching. The **Teaching notes** suggest possible ways that you can explain, demonstrate and discuss the feature to develop understanding. Sessions often involve some oral composition or shared writing, with the pupils involved in suggesting ideas and correcting mistakes.

The main teaching session covers the objectives that are required for the pupils to work at the expected standard, but there is also a suggestion for how you can **Extend** the focus for pupils who have grasped the main concept and are ready to delve deeper. These suggestions often provide a bridge to later lessons in the programme.

PRACTISE

Following the teaching session, the pupils are ready to practise the grammar or punctuation feature that has been introduced and clear page references are provided for the corresponding lesson in the pupil book. This provides the pupils with rich practice activities to consolidate their learning. The pupils can work individually or in pairs. In paired work, discussion between partners can help to develop understanding, encourage thoughtful answers and promote oral rehearsal.

At the top of each pupil book page a **Remember** panel provides a child-friendly summary of a key learning point from the lesson with examples that refer back to the **Focus text**. This acts as a reminder for the pupil and is also a useful reference for parents if sections of the pupil book are set as homework.

In **Grammar 5**, there are three pupil book activities for each lesson. The first **Try it** activity is designed to check that the pupils understand the key learning point; the second is designed to develop and use this understanding within sentences. You could do some of the activities orally, with the class or in groups, before the pupils write their answers. Each lesson then ends with a **Sentence practice** activity where the pupils compose their own sentence or sentences using the concept that has been taught in the lesson. If a pupil requires additional challenge, the **Sentence practice** could be extended by increasing the number of sentences required. A sample page from the pupil book is provided on page 7. It shows the structure of a typical page and some of the main features.

As the pupil book is completed, it will form an ongoing record of the pupil's progress. It will also be a useful reminder for the pupil when writing independently.

Answers to all the pupil book activities are provided in the teacher's guide. Alongside the answers you will also find detailed annotations offering guidance on what to look out for and how to tackle potential problems, as well as suggestions for discussing or comparing pupils' answers.

There are **Revision** pages at the end of each section of the pupil book. In **Grammar 5**, these pages revise concepts introduced in earlier books as well as material from earlier sections of the current book, making sure that learning is not forgotten. The focus of each revision activity is given on the **Answers** pages in the teacher's guide to help you identify areas where the pupils might need further revision.

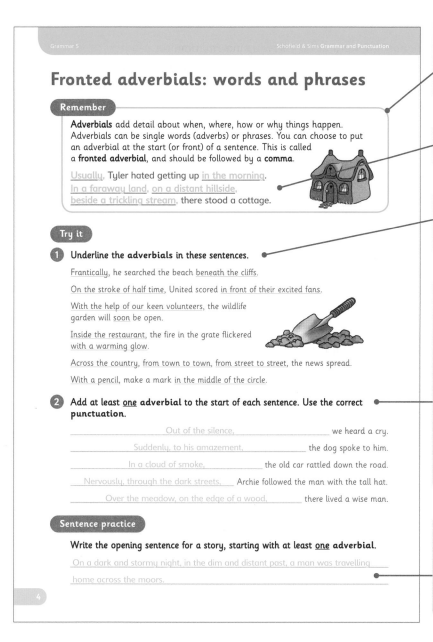

The **Remember** panels provide a child-friendly summary of the key learning point for the page.

Examples are given that refer back to the **Focus text**.

The first **Try it** activity checks for understanding of the key learning point.

The second **Try it** activity develops the pupils' understanding and allows them to practise using the new learning in context.
You could do some of these activities orally before the pupils write their own answers [e.g. orally rehearsing sentences or discussing choice of words].

Each lesson ends with **Sentence practice**, where the pupils compose their own sentence or sentences using the key learning point.

APPLY

A challenge when teaching grammar and punctuation is ensuring that pupils transfer learning from grammar lessons into their own writing. This is why the **Teaching notes** always provide a list of suggestions for activities where the pupils might apply their new learning in written, or sometimes oral, composition. These opportunities may be in English lessons or across the curriculum. You can use these suggestions as and when appropriate and you should also look for opportunities to embed learning in the writing activities you already have planned.

It is important to establish the expectation that what has been taught and practised in a grammar and punctuation lesson is applied when writing. This can be helped by setting targets for writing that relate to a specific grammar and punctuation concept that has been taught, and referring to these before, during and after writing, especially in marking and feedback. You will find further support for target-setting on page 9.

At the end of each section of the pupil book there is a short **Writing task**. This again helps to make explicit the link between the grammar and punctuation lessons and the pupils' own writing. The **Writing task** provides an opportunity for pupils to apply, or 'show off', what they have learnt about grammar and punctuation by using it in written composition. It can be used as a starting point for further creative writing or topic-based activities. There is more information about how to use and assess the **Writing task** on page 8.

ASSESS

Regular assessment is crucial to check understanding, reflect on learning and monitor progress. It is important that teachers know what the pupils have learnt, what they are finding difficult and what they need to know next. This helps inform teaching, planning and target-setting. **Grammar 5** and its related **Teacher's Guide** offer frequent opportunities and a range of resources for in-school assessment, which can be used flexibly in line with your own school's assessment policy.

Ongoing assessment

At the end of each page of the **Teaching notes** you will find a short assessment task based around a dictation exercise. This is designed to be used once the pupils have completed the relevant lesson in the pupil book and begun to apply the new learning in their writing. The pupils are required to write and punctuate dictated sentences. They are often then asked to change or annotate the sentences in some way, following verbal prompts. This dictation task is designed to show whether pupils have understood the terminology and the key learning objective of the lesson. Sometimes previous learning is also checked. A **Dictation assessment shee**t is available to download from the Schofield & Sims website.

Periodic assessment

The **Writing task** at the end of each section in the pupil book allows for a more formal assessment of how the pupils are applying their cumulative knowledge of sentence structure, grammar and punctuation in their own writing.

At Key Stage 2, the writing tasks require pupils to write for different purposes and in different forms. You can remind the pupils that you will be looking at their choices of vocabulary, grammar and punctuation but do not give any further help or examples of sentences, words or phrases that might affect the assessment. Allow the pupils a few minutes' planning time to note down their ideas before they begin writing.

Included in the teacher's guide is an **Analysis sheet** for each **Writing task** [pages 32, 56 and 80]. This lists relevant criteria relating to punctuation, and to grammar and sentence structure based on what has been taught to date. Look for each criterion in the pupil's completed **Writing task** and record whether there is no evidence, some evidence or clear evidence of the use of that feature in the piece of writing. Photocopies of these sheets can also be used to analyse other samples of writing to give a better picture of a pupil's abilities.

Also included is a **Pupil checklist** for each **Writing task** [pages 33, 57 and 81]. This is designed to encourage pupils' self-assessment and also allows you to give targeted feedback. As the pupils complete the checklist you could ask them to annotate their writing to show where they have successfully used a particular grammar or punctuation feature [e.g. circling the conjunctions they have used].

Whether you choose to use the **Analysis sheet** or the **Pupil checklist**, both include a space for you to record a future target for the pupil. This is an important part of the writing assessments: identifying strengths and weaknesses and informing future teaching. Any problems or misunderstandings that are noted should be addressed and targets updated based on the evidence.

Summative assessment

There is a **Final test** provided as a photocopiable resource on pages 82–85 of this teacher's guide. This is designed to be used as an end-of-year assessment when all or most of the sections of the pupil book are complete. It is similar in style to the short answer test in the end of Key Stage 2 National Tests and it covers all the content introduced in the programme so far. You can use it to help check the pupils' learning and whether their progress is in line with expectations.

A **Mark scheme** for the **Final test** is provided on pages 86–87 and gives the answers and assessment focus of each question. The **Analysis sheet** for the **Final test** allows you to record the pupils' marks and will be helpful in identifying individual or class strengths and areas that might need to be revisited. This can be found on page 88 and a whole-class version is available to download from the Schofield & Sims website.

Tracking progress

A number of resources are provided at the back of the teacher's guide and as downloadable resources to further support assessment of learning, tracking progress and record-keeping.

Following a **Writing task**, if a group of pupils require further focused support on a particular writing target, the **Target tracking sheet** on page 89 can be used to note evidence of progress towards that target. You should look for evidence of progress in independent writing in English and in other subjects. Judgements should not be made solely on one piece of writing.

Pupil name	Evidence from independent writing	Progress in independent writing
Sarah Jacobs	Paragraph on 'My family'. Book review of 'The Nightingale'. Science report on 'Habitats'.	1 2 3

The target should be reviewed after a set period of time to see if it has been achieved. A new target might then be set, or further teaching and reinforcement opportunities planned as necessary. A **Pupil target reminder** is available to download from the Schofield & Sims website. This can be placed on a pupil's desk as a prompt to remind them of their current writing target.

The **Learning pathways sheet** on page 90 acts as an at-a-glance overview of where a pupil is in their learning. If completed at regular intervals [e.g. at the end of every term] it allows you to track the progress that has been made and to identify areas where further support might be needed. Alternatively, it can be completed just once at the end of the year to act as a useful summative record for the pupil's subsequent teacher. The chart shows criteria in line with the expected standards for Year 5. Circles are ticked to show the depth of a pupil's understanding. These judgements should be made using a variety of evidence, including a number of examples of independent writing. Learning is only definitely embedded when the concept is always or nearly always present, based on evidence from a range of writing tasks. A **Learning pathways class chart**, available to download from the Schofield & Sims website, allows you to keep a record of progress for the whole class in one spreadsheet.

The pupils should also be encouraged to reflect on their own learning at regular intervals, saying what they have learnt and how they have used it in their writing. There is a **Progress chart** at the back of the pupil book where the pupils can record their progress through the programme by ticking the circle when they feel they have achieved the content of the statement.

Lesson 1 Fronted adverbials: words and phrases

> Focus using fronted adverbials [words and phrases] to add detail and for effect
>
> Key terms adverbial, adverb, phrase, comma
>
> Focus text Usually, Tyler hated getting up in the morning.
> In a faraway land, on a distant hillside, beside a trickling stream, there stood a cottage.
> Gradually, the green smoke cleared.
> Jane was extremely worried about her son.

TEACH

Show the focus text. Explain that these are the opening sentences for four stories. Read and discuss each sentence [e.g. how it draws the reader into the story]. Ask: What makes it intriguing or effective?

Identify and underline the main clause in each sentence [Tyler hated getting up; there stood a cottage; the green smoke cleared; Jane was extremely worried]. Ask the pupils to name the other parts of the sentences [e.g. they are adverbials – adverbs and phrases that tell us more about the event in the main clause].

Discuss what details these adverbials add to the sentences [e.g. details about time – *when* Tyler hated getting up; place – *where* the cottage stood; manner – *how* the smoke cleared; cause – *why* Jane was worried]. Explain that an adverb can also be used to strengthen an adjective [e.g. <u>extremely</u> worried].

Point out that adverbials are often deliberately placed at the start of a sentence, to vary sentence openings or for effect. Discuss the three instances of this in the focus text: how in the first sentence, 'usually' suggests today might be different; how the three fronted adverbials in the second sentence slowly focus in on a place; and how 'gradually' in the third sentence builds tension and suspense.

Invite the pupils to orally compose or write some more opening sentences for stories, using a sentence from the focus text as a model [e.g. In a field, beneath a tree, in a hole in the ground, there lived a ...]. Remind them that commas are used after fronted adverbials. When more than one adverbial is added to the start of a sentence, the 'list' of adverbials is separated using commas.

EXTEND Discuss the use of adverbs with adverbials [e.g. <u>only</u> in the morning; <u>really</u> slowly].

PRACTISE

Pupil book page 4

APPLY

- In stories, the pupils use fronted adverbials to show character [e.g. Enthusiastically, ...; Shyly, ...] or to emphasise feelings [e.g. Confidently, ...; Nervously, ...; Patiently, ...].
- Encourage the use of fronted adverbials to add a touch of drama or surprise [e.g. To his amazement ...].
- The pupils use fronted adverbials in instructions or information texts to add detail or for variety [e.g. With a pencil, carefully draw ...; Throughout Britain, ...; During the colder winter months, ...].

ASSESS

Dictation: <u>With a heavy heart</u>, he entered the tunnel. <u>Cautiously</u>, he groped his way through the twisting maze. <u>In the distance</u>, there was the roar of a monster.
Say: Underline all the fronted adverbials.
Check: There is a comma after each fronted adverbial.

Pupil book answers

Fronted adverbials: words and phrases

Remember

Adverbials add detail about when, where, how or why things happen. Adverbials can be single words (adverbs) or phrases. You can choose to put an adverbial at the start (or front) of a sentence. This is called a **fronted adverbial**, and should be followed by a **comma**.

Usually, Tyler hated getting up in the morning.
In a faraway land, on a distant hillside, beside a trickling stream, there stood a cottage.

Try it

1 Underline the **adverbials** in these sentences.

Frantically, he searched the beach beneath the cliffs.

On the stroke of half time, United scored in front of their excited fans.

With the help of our keen volunteers, the wildlife garden will soon be open.

Inside the restaurant, the fire in the grate flickered with a warming glow.

Across the country, from town to town, from street to street, the news spread.

With a pencil, make a mark in the middle of the circle.

2 Add at least **one** adverbial to the start of each sentence. Use the correct punctuation.

_____ Out of the silence, _____ we heard a cry.

_____ Suddenly, to his amazement, _____ the dog spoke to him.

_____ In a cloud of smoke, _____ the old car rattled down the road.

_____ Nervously, through the dark streets, _____ Archie followed the man with the tall hat.

_____ Over the meadow, on the edge of a wood, _____ there lived a wise man.

Sentence practice

Write the opening sentence for a story, starting with at least **one** adverbial.

On a dark and stormy night, in the dim and distant past, a man was travelling home across the moors.

Check that the pupils have underlined all the adverbials [e.g. soon], and not just those at the start of the sentence.

If the pupils have difficulty identifying the adverbials, help them to first identify the main clause – the part that makes sense independently.

Explain that 'in the grate' should not be underlined as it is not an adverbial here. It is a prepositional phrase describing a noun [the fire], so it is part of the noun phrase.

These are just examples. Although any adverbial is acceptable, encourage the pupils to try out different ideas, thinking about the effect achieved. Compare their choices. Some pupils may have added more than one adverbial to the start of a sentence, following the model in the focus text.

Each fronted adverbial must be followed by a comma.

Again, this is just an example of an opening sentence using two fronted adverbials. Any adverbial[s] could be used but there should be some evidence that the pupils have thought about the effect created. Compare and discuss their choices.

The fronted adverbial must be followed by a comma.

Lesson 2 Fronted adverbials: clauses

Focus using fronted adverbials [subordinate clauses] beginning with a range of conjunctions

Key terms main clause, adverbial, subordinate clause, conjunction

Focus text **For a moment, as the lightning lit up the night, she saw a figure in the doorway. Although it was just a glimpse, Abbie thought it was him. She needed to get closer so that she could be sure.**

TEACH

Show the focus text. Discuss what sort of story it might be taken from [e.g. an adventure story].

Ask the pupils to identify the main clause – the part that makes sense by itself – in each sentence. Underline them [she saw a figure, Abbie thought it was him, She needed to get closer]. Ask the pupils to tell you about the other parts of the sentences [e.g. the use of subordinate clauses, starting with conjunctions – as, although, so that – to add more detail]. Help the pupils to distinguish between the different types of adverbial in the first sentence: phrases [for a moment, in the doorway] and clauses [as the lightning lit up the night]. Remind them that a clause must have a subject and a verb.

Explain that these subordinate clauses function as adverbials. Like all adverbials, they tell us more about the action or event in the main clause. Adverbials that are subordinate clauses start with a subordinating conjunction. The choice of conjunction is important because it shows how the adverbial develops the idea in the main clause [e.g. in the first sentence, 'as' links two events by *time*; in the second sentence, 'although' *contrasts* two events; in the third sentence, 'so that' gives a reason *why*].

Explain that subordinate clauses, like other adverbials, can be placed at the start of a sentence for variation or for effect. For example, in the first sentence, starting with adverbials [a phrase and then a clause] helps to build up to the moment when Abbie sees the figure; in the second sentence, the fronted adverbial [a clause] emphasises that it was just a glimpse. Remind the pupils to use a comma after a fronted adverbial.

Invite the pupils to reorder the third sentence so that it begins with the adverbial [So that she could be sure, she needed ...]. Discuss whether this sounds more or less effective than in the focus text.

EXTEND Discuss other conjunctions that are used to contrast ideas [e.g. though; whereas].

PRACTISE

Pupil book page 5

APPLY

- Encourage the pupils to collect conjunctions when reading. They then use these conjunctions when writing, to link clauses and start sentences [e.g. even though; whenever; as long as].
- The pupils write stories, using oral rehearsal to decide when to use a fronted subordinate clause.
- The pupils use fronted subordinate clauses in non-fiction texts, such as sports reports [e.g. Until City scored in the eightieth minute, it was another dull game.] or instructions [e.g. When it is ready, ...].

ASSESS

Dictation: In her comfortable bed, Milly slept as the sun crept over the horizon. Though voices drifted up from the street below, she still did not wake. When her mother called her, she did not stir.

Say: Underline all the fronted subordinate clauses.

Check: The fronted adverbial [a phrase] and non-fronted subordinate clause in the first sentence are not underlined. There is a comma after each fronted adverbial.

Pupil book answers

Fronted adverbials: clauses

Remember

Subordinate clauses start with a **conjunction** and function as **adverbials**.
Subordinate clauses tell you more about the event in the **main clause**. You can
put the subordinate clause before the main clause. These fronted subordinate
clauses, like other fronted adverbials, are followed by a **comma**.

As the lightning lit up the night, she saw a figure in the doorway.
Although it was just a glimpse, Abbie thought it was him.

Try it

1 Underline the **subordinate clause** in each sentence. Circle the **conjunction**.

(Although) it was raining, the air was still warm.

In the morning, he gave her a map (so that) she could find her way.

(Once) we have the money, we will buy new equipment for the gym.

(Whenever) I leave the room, you start misbehaving.

(Since) it was time for lunch, she ran home.

Check that the adverbials underlined are subordinate clauses rather than phrases [e.g. not 'In the morning'].

This exercise introduces some new words that can be used as conjunctions.

2 Rewrite each sentence so that it begins with the **subordinate clause**.
Punctuate it correctly.

The visitor paused for a moment before he spoke to the class.

 Before he spoke to the class, the visitor paused for a moment.

George could not rest while his father was in danger.

 While his father was in danger, George could not rest.

The children climbed over the fence although they weren't really allowed in the garden.

 Although they weren't really allowed in the garden, the children climbed over
 the fence.

Check that sentences have been correctly punctuated with a comma after the fronted subordinate clause.

Discuss the effect of re-ordering the sentences [e.g. emphasising the fact that the children were not allowed, or that George's father was in danger].

Sentence practice

Write **three** sentences using the **main clause** below. Start each sentence with a different **subordinate clause**.

… she went through the gate.

 As it was open, she went through the gate.

 While no-one was looking, she went through the gate.

 Although she knew it was wrong, she went through the gate.

5

This is just an example of three different correctly punctuated sentences starting
with subordinate clauses as adverbials. Each sentence should use a different
conjunction. You could compare the pupils' answers, discussing how the choice
of conjunction develops the idea in different ways – for example, giving a reason
[e.g. as]; linking events by time [e.g. while] or contrasting two ideas [e.g. although].

Lesson 3 Punctuating direct speech

Focus punctuating direct speech when spoken words are split by non-spoken words

Key terms direct speech, inverted commas, comma

Focus text "Did you hear that scratching sound?" asked Maya, springing to her feet.
"It sounds like rats in the cellar," said Dylan. "There are probably hundreds of them down there."
"I heard it before," said Maya, "but this time it's louder."

TEACH

Display the focus text. Ask the pupils how they know this is direct speech [e.g. the use of inverted commas; the layout on the page]. Read the focus text aloud using appropriate expression. Discuss ideas about the events and characters [e.g. Where could they be? What might happen next?].

Use the first line of the focus text to recap how inverted commas are used to punctuate direct speech [e.g. they are placed at the beginning and end of spoken words; the punctuation at the end of the spoken words is placed *inside* the inverted commas].

Explain that sometimes we use 'said …', to split the spoken words. For example, when Dylan speaks, he says two sentences, and 'said Dylan' is placed between the two sentences. Discuss the punctuation used in this situation. The first spoken sentence is punctuated as normal with a comma separating the spoken words from 'said Dylan'. The full stop after 'said Dylan' shows that it is the end of a sentence. The second spoken sentence is then added in a second set of inverted commas. It begins with a capital letter and ends with a full stop, again placed *inside* the inverted commas.

Discuss the last sentence of the focus text. Explain that here Maya says only one sentence – we can tell it is only one sentence because it continues 'but'. Discuss how the punctuation is different this time. There is a comma rather than a full stop after 'said Maya', and the spoken sentence continues in the second set of speech marks with a lower-case letter ['b' in 'but'] rather than a capital letter.

EXTEND Discuss how to combine action with direct speech [e.g. asked Maya, springing to her feet].

PRACTISE

Pupil book page 6

APPLY

- The pupils choose a place in a story where direct speech could be used to advance the action [e.g. introducing a new problem]. They then write a short dialogue, varying the position of 'said X'.
- When writing stories, the pupils use direct speech to show character. Encourage them to include details with the reporting clause that show what a character is doing when speaking [e.g. "No," he muttered, shaking his head. "I will not do it."].
- The pupils use a line of direct speech to open or close a story. They split the spoken words with the reporting clause [e.g. "Well," said Harry, "I never expected that."].

ASSESS

Dictation: "What are you doing this weekend?" asked Molly.
"I'm going to visit my Aunt Kate," said Emily, "and we are going shopping."
"That sounds like fun," sighed Molly. "I'm stuck at home."
Check: The direct speech is correctly set out and punctuated.

Pupil book answers

Punctuating direct speech

Remember

In **direct speech**, the spoken words are sometimes split up, with 'said X' in the middle of them. If someone says two complete sentences, you put a full stop between the sentences.

"It sounds like rats," said Dylan. "There are probably hundreds of them down there."

If someone says one sentence, you put a comma after 'said X' to show that the sentence continues.

"I heard it before," said Maya, "but this time it's louder."

Try it

1. Read this **direct speech** and decide if there is <u>one</u> spoken sentence or <u>two</u>. Then add the missing **punctuation**.

    "Take care of yourself," she shouted. "Those roads can be dangerous."

    "We must find the wise man," said the chief, "and ask him what to do."

    "You stay here," said Arjun, "while we go inside."

    "It's not my fault," Natalie said quickly. "I was only trying to help."

    "You should hurry," said the ticket inspector, "because the train is leaving in a few minutes."

2. Complete the sentence spoken by each character and add the **punctuation**.

    "I'm having a party," announced Kayla, "and <u>I want you all to come."</u>

    "I've looked everywhere," moaned Louie, "but <u>I still can't find my book."</u>

    "When it stops raining," said Sarah, <u>"we will go for a run."</u>

    "We are going to the cinema," explained Lucy, "so <u>I have to hurry home."</u>

    "We should stay here," insisted Nisha, "or <u>Dad will never find us in this crowd."</u>

Sentence practice

Freya and Lee are trapped. Write <u>two</u> lines of **direct speech**, split up as above, to show this.

<u>"We must get out of here," whispered Lee, "before the thieves come back."</u>

<u>"Good idea," said Freya. "Let's get to the door and make a run for it."</u>

6

Encourage the pupils to look at the examples above to check that they have punctuated the sentences correctly.

Remind them that if the spoken words continue with a conjunction [and, while, because], then it is one sentence and should be punctuated accordingly. Check that the final full stop is added inside the inverted commas.

Different pupils will have completed the sentences in different ways, but it should be a plausible continuation of the spoken sentence.

Answers should be punctuated as one sentence. Check that both parts of the sentence are punctuated correctly.

This is an example of two suitable lines of direct speech. Look for direct speech where the spoken words are split by 'said X', as practised on this page. Check that it is punctuated correctly.

Lesson 4   Direct and indirect speech

> Focus   introducing indirect speech and comparing it to direct speech
>
> Key terms   direct speech, **indirect speech [reported speech]**, punctuation, inverted commas
>
> Focus text   Megan said that she couldn't come.
> "What are we going to do now?" snapped Greg.
> Yasmin suggested that we ask Zara. Jamal said that we could manage on our own.

TEACH

Show the focus text and read it aloud. Discuss the conversation between the characters. Ask: Is it direct speech? [The second sentence is direct speech – we can tell from the use of inverted commas – but the other sentences are not, even though they tell us what someone said.]

Explain that the other sentences in the focus text use indirect speech [also called reported speech]. Explain that indirect speech is when we write what someone said without using the actual spoken words. Indirect speech does not need the inverted commas and punctuation used in direct speech.

Explain that we use indirect speech because long sections of direct speech can be boring. Indirect speech can quickly summarise what is said. We can keep direct speech for the most important parts of a dialogue, so that it has greater impact [e.g. Greg's angry response].

Discuss how the lines of indirect speech begin, noting the use of the word 'that' after the verb [e.g. Megan said that …]. Explain that this is often omitted [e.g. Megan said she couldn't come.].

With the pupils, change a line of indirect speech to direct speech, discussing changes in wording and punctuation [e.g. "We could ask Zara," suggested Yasmin. "We can manage on our own," said Jamal.]. Then change the line of direct speech into indirect speech [e.g. Greg asked what we were going to do now.]. Point out the change in tense here – the direct speech is in the present tense; the indirect speech is in the past tense to match the reporting clause [snapped Greg].

EXTEND   Experiment with changing a variety of sentences from direct to indirect speech, discussing the changes to tense, pronouns and wording [e.g. "Will you come?"/He asked if we would come.].

PRACTISE

Pupil book page 7

APPLY

- When they are writing, challenge the pupils to limit their use of direct speech, using some indirect speech instead.
- When writing a story, the pupils look for an opportunity to use indirect speech to contrast what a character says and does or thinks [e.g. He said that he was going home but instead he hid outside.].
- The pupils use indirect speech when writing a summary of a story [e.g. The serpent told her that …].
- When writing newspaper reports, the pupils use indirect speech as well as direct quotes [e.g. Sergeant Hobson went on to tell the audience …].

ASSESS

Dictation: "We are starting our new topic today," said Mr Branston. "It is about China."
Say: Rewrite this as indirect speech.
Answer: e.g. Mr Branston said that we were starting a new topic about China.
Check: The punctuation is correct in both the direct and indirect speech.

Pupil book answers

Schofield & Sims **Grammar and Punctuation**   Grammar 5

Direct and indirect speech

Remember

Direct speech records the actual words that are spoken, by putting them in **inverted commas**.

Megan said, "I can't come."

Indirect speech (also called **reported speech**) records what has been said without using the actual words spoken. No inverted commas are needed.

Megan said that she couldn't come.

Try it

1. Write whether each sentence shows **direct speech** or **indirect speech**. If it is direct speech, add the missing **punctuation**.

   She said that she hated singing in assembly.   _indirect speech_

   Jason shouted, "Let's get out of here!"   _direct speech_

   Bella told us that the hall was flooded.   _indirect speech_

   Elijah agreed that we were right.   _indirect speech_

   Mum sighed, "I think that is a very bad idea."   _direct speech_

Check that inverted commas and other punctuation marks are used correctly in the sentences using direct speech.

2. Complete the boxes so that each sentence is written as **direct speech** and then as **indirect speech**. Punctuate your answers correctly.

Direct speech	Indirect speech
Mrs Shah said, "Everyone go home."	Mrs Shah told everyone to go home.
He shouted to us, "Follow that car!"	He shouted to us to follow the car.
"Are you busy?" she asked.	She asked if we were busy.
"You can help if you want to," said Dad.	Dad said that we could help if we wanted to.

The wording does not need to be exactly as shown but it should not significantly change the meaning of the original sentence.

Check that both types of sentence are punctuated correctly.

Sentence practice

Ross tells his mum that he is going to Amit's house. Write his mum's reply using **indirect speech**.

Mum said that he must be back by six.   7

This is just an example of a sentence using indirect speech.

17

Lesson 5 Pronouns

Focus identifying pronouns by their function; introducing different types of pronoun

Key terms pronoun, possessive pronoun, noun, noun phrase, personal pronoun

Focus text A man was walking along a country lane when he saw something on the ground – a handful of sparkling beads. He picked them up. "Well, look at these," he said to himself. "Someone must have dropped them." He saw an old lady ahead of him and he thought he would ask if they were hers.

TEACH

Show the focus text and read it aloud. Discuss what type of story it might be [e.g. folk tale].

Ask the pupils what type of word is highlighted and why they have been used [pronouns – words that take the place of nouns or noun phrases to avoid repetition – e.g. 'he' in place of 'a man']. Ask: What does 'them' or 'these' refer to? How do we know? Underline the noun phrases that the pronouns refer to [a man, a handful of sparkling beads, an old lady].

Explain that there are different types of pronoun, some of which are used in the focus text. For example, there are personal pronouns, which are the ones we use most frequently [e.g. he; she; they; him; her; them]. There are also possessive pronouns that show ownership [e.g. mine; yours; theirs]. Ask the pupils to identify the possessive pronoun in the focus text ['hers' – meaning the old lady's].

Circle the word 'these'. Explain that 'these' is used as a pronoun here because it takes the place of a noun ['these' = the beads]. If it said 'these beads', then 'these' would be a determiner.

The focus text introduces two new types of pronoun: reflexive pronouns, which refer back to the subject [e.g. he said to himself], and indefinite pronouns [e.g. something; someone]. Discuss the use of the indefinite pronouns in the focus text [e.g. What nouns do they refer to?]. Explain that these pronouns stand in place of an unknown noun – one not mentioned yet or as yet unknown. [Note: The pupils do not need to know the terms for reflexive and indefinite pronouns. They just need to recognise that they function as pronouns: they are used in place of a noun.]

EXTEND Introduce the relative pronouns 'who', 'which', 'that' [e.g. He was the one who found them.]. [Note: Relative pronouns are covered in Lesson 13.]

PRACTISE

Pupil book page 8

APPLY

- When writing stories, the pupils use indefinite pronouns [e.g. someone; something; somebody] to create suspense [e.g. Somebody was coming up the stairs.].
- When writing non-fiction texts, the pupils use words such as 'this'/'that' and 'these'/'those' as pronouns to avoid repeating words or phrases [e.g This/That is why …].
- When they are editing, encourage the pupils to use pronouns to avoid repetition.

ASSESS

Dictation: Adam said someone had knocked his drink over but we know that he spilt it himself. I know it was his because I saw him pour it.
Say: Underline all the pronouns and circle the possessive pronoun.
Check: The determiner 'his' in 'his drink' is not underlined. [Recap the difference, if need be, between the two instances of 'his' in the text.]

Pupil book answers

Pronouns

Remember

There are many different types of **pronoun** but they all have the same function – they stand in place of **nouns** or noun phrases.

<u>A man</u> was walking along when he saw something on the ground – <u>a handful of sparkling beads</u>. He picked them up. "Well, look at these," he said to himself. "Someone must have dropped them."

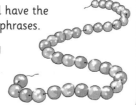

Try it

1. Underline all the **pronouns** in each sentence.

   Mum made <u>herself</u> a cup of tea and poured <u>us</u> some juice.

   Rose ran away when <u>she</u> heard <u>something</u> moving in the woods.

   That ice cream looks delicious. Can <u>I</u> have <u>some</u>?

   <u>We</u> organised the event <u>ourselves</u> and <u>it</u> was a great success.

   <u>They</u> looked at all the paintings and decided <u>mine</u> was the best.

   If <u>you</u> give <u>her</u> the seeds, Lucia can plant <u>them</u> <u>herself</u>.

2. Rewrite each sentence using **pronouns** instead of the underlined nouns and noun phrases.

   <u>This workbook</u> is <u>your workbook</u> and <u>that workbook</u> is <u>my workbook</u>.

   This is yours and that is mine.

   <u>Scott</u> was annoyed with <u>Scott</u> when <u>Scott</u> missed <u>the open goal</u>.

   He was annoyed with himself when he missed it.

   <u>An unknown person</u> was coming so <u>Anish and I</u> hastily put <u>the letters</u> back.

   Someone was coming so we hastily put them back.

Sentence practice

Write a sentence using the **pronouns** 'someone' and 'himself'.

Someone had left a skateboard in the hall and Dad fell over it and hurt himself.

8

Check that all the pronouns have been underlined. You could discuss which noun each one refers to.

The word 'some' is used as a pronoun in the third sentence ['some' = ice cream] but not in the first sentence, where it is a determiner [some juice]. You may wish to discuss this with the pupils. [Note: This will be covered in Lesson 27.]

You could discuss the effect of using the pronouns [e.g. briefer; less repetitious; more effective].

This is just an example of a sentence using the two given pronouns. The sentence could also include other pronouns.

Lesson 6 Pronouns and ambiguity

Focus recognising ambiguity in the use of pronouns; rewording sentences to clarify pronoun references

Key terms pronoun, **ambiguity**

Focus text Although it was old, Aaron still rode his bike every day.
When Aaron rode his bike into the fence, he badly damaged it.

TEACH

Show the first sentence of the focus text. Read the sentence and discuss the use of the pronoun 'it'. Ask: What noun does 'it' refer to? [Aaron's bike] How do we know? [It is mentioned in the second part of the sentence.] Explain that although pronouns usually refer *back* to a noun already mentioned, they can also refer *forward* to something mentioned later in the sentence, as here.

Show the second sentence. Read it aloud and discuss what noun 'it' refers to – is it the bike or the fence? Explain that here the use of the pronoun is confusing because it gives the sentence two possible meanings [either he damaged the bike or he damaged the fence].

Remind the pupils that we use pronouns to avoid repeating nouns or noun phrases. However, it must be clear which noun or noun phrase a pronoun refers to. In the first sentence, the meaning is clear because there is only one noun that 'it' could refer to. In the second sentence, however, the word 'it' could refer to more than one noun so the meaning of the sentence is unclear. Introduce the term 'ambiguity' to describe a situation where there is uncertainty or more than one possible meaning.

Explain that it is important to recognise ambiguity and then to fix it – i.e. to make the meaning clear. One way of making the meaning clear is to replace the pronoun with the original noun [e.g. he badly damaged the bike/the fence], but this could lead to clumsy repetition of words.

Another way of making the meaning clear is to reorder or reword the sentence. Discuss how to reorder the sentence about Aaron, splitting up the two nouns so that the pronoun 'it' could only refer to one of them [e.g. Aaron badly damaged his bike when he rode it into the fence.]. There are other ways of rewording the sentence [e.g. When Aaron rode into the fence, he badly damaged his bike.].

EXTEND Discuss ambiguous pronouns in indirect speech [e.g. 'Oscar told Aaron that his bike was old.' – whose bike?]. Show that direct speech could make this clearer [e.g. Oscar said, "My bike is old."].

PRACTISE

Pupil book page 9

APPLY

- The pupils practise constructing sentences with a pronoun that refers *forward* to something mentioned later in the sentence [e.g. Although she was scared, Lucy ...; Although it is dormant, the volcano ...].
- When they are writing, encourage the pupils to reread sentences and passages, checking that their use of pronouns is clear.
- When they are editing, encourage the pupils to check for ambiguous pronouns. They then work in pairs to decide how to fix the problem [e.g. replace the pronoun with the noun; use a synonymous noun; reword the sentence].

ASSESS

Dictation: Megan and Erin saw Josh and Max when they were outside the cinema.
Say: Rewrite this sentence so that the meaning is clear.
Answer: e.g. Megan and Erin were outside the cinema when they saw Josh and Max.

Pupil book answers

Pronouns and ambiguity

Remember

You can use **pronouns** to avoid repeating **nouns** or noun phrases. However, it must be clear which noun or noun phrase a pronoun refers to.

When Aaron rode <u>his bike</u> into <u>the fence</u>, he badly damaged it. (meaning is unclear or ambiguous)
Aaron badly damaged <u>his bike</u> when he rode it into <u>the fence</u>. (meaning is clear)

Try it

1 Which <u>two</u> **nouns** could the underlined **pronoun** in each sentence refer to?

If I take the model off the stand, it will be easier to mend <u>it</u>.

___model___ or ___stand___

When the hunters went to catch the stags, <u>they</u> ran away.

___hunters___ or ___stags___

When Dad dropped the computer on his leg, <u>it</u> broke.

___computer___ or ___leg___

I saw her picture in a magazine but now I can't find <u>it</u>.

___picture___ or ___magazine___

The police told the passengers that <u>they</u> would be there for some time.

___police___ or ___passengers___

2 Now rewrite the sentences above, keeping the **pronoun** but making clear which **noun** it refers to.

It will be easier to mend the model if I take it off the stand.

As soon as they saw the stags, the hunters ran away.

Dad broke his leg when he dropped the computer on it.

I can't find the picture of her that I saw in the magazine.

The police said that the passengers would be there for some time.

Sentence practice

Write a sentence using the **nouns** 'rabbit' and 'hat' and the **pronoun** 'it'.

The rabbit disappeared when the magician put it in the hat.

9

The pupils may have reworded the sentences in different ways to resolve the ambiguity. They may also have chosen to make the pronoun refer to the other noun [e.g. 'mend the stand' rather than 'the model'].

However, they should not just replace the pronoun with the noun, making the sentence more repetitive [e.g. not 'If I take the model off the stand, it will be easier to mend <u>the model</u>.'].

This is an example of a sentence using the two nouns and the pronoun. It should be clear which noun the pronoun refers to, the rabbit or the hat [e.g. 'When the magician put the rabbit in the hat, it disappeared.' could be ambiguous].

Lesson 7 Verbs: auxiliary verbs

Focus   using verb forms with auxiliary verbs [e.g. progressive and perfect forms]

Key terms   past tense, present tense, verb, progressive form, perfect form, **auxiliary verb**

Focus text   United <u>have been</u> woeful all season and this <u>was</u> another dismal performance. Until Johnson <u>scored</u>, a goal <u>did not look</u> likely. Then Allan <u>crossed</u> the ball and Johnson <u>was waiting</u> at the far post to <u>nod</u> home. Now, United <u>will face</u> City in the next round.

TEACH

Display the focus text and read it aloud. Discuss what happened during the match – and what the report tells us about events before [e.g. United have been woeful] and in the future [they will face City].

Explain that there are two main tenses: past and present tense. Simple past or present tense requires just one verb – for example, 'scored' and 'crossed' are simple past tense verbs. However, there are other verb forms that require 'helper' verbs to go before the main verb. These helper verbs are called auxiliary verbs. Ask the pupils to identify verbs in the focus text with a main verb and an auxiliary verb [e.g. have been; was waiting]. Circle the auxiliary verbs [have, did, was, will].

The pupils should already be familiar with some of these verb forms. Ask them to find an example of the past progressive form in the focus text [was waiting]. Remind the pupils that the past progressive form uses the auxiliary verbs 'was'/'were' and shows that an action was in progress for some time. Ask the pupils to find an example of the perfect form of a verb [have been]. The perfect form uses the auxiliary verb 'have'/'has' and refers here to an event that continues into the present. [Note: The past perfect verb form is introduced in the next lesson, Lesson 8.]

Point out that the focus text refers to an event in the future [United will face …]. Explain that we can use the auxiliary verb 'will' with the present tense of the main verb to refer to the future.

Look at how the auxiliary verbs 'do'/'does'/'did' are used to make a negative statement [e.g. 'A goal looked likely.' – positive statement; 'A goal <u>did not</u> look likely.' – negative statement].

EXTEND   Discuss other ways in which we can refer to future time [e.g. United will be facing City in the next round. United are going to face City in the next round. United face City in the next round.].

PRACTISE

Pupil book page 10

APPLY

- The pupils write news reports, using a range of verb forms to refer to events [e.g. were waiting to hear; have been known]. They end their reports by referring to future events.
- The pupils write an 'autobiography' referring to the past, present and future. They use auxiliary verbs to refer to different times [e.g. I have been …; Now I am …; Next year I will …].
- The pupils write a letter from a character in a story. They use verb forms to refer to past events and/or the future [e.g. I have found a golden egg. I am hiding it under my bed. I will sell it later.].

ASSESS

Dictation: I am writing to you to say sorry. I realise I <u>have</u> forgotten your birthday. I <u>did</u> not know it was on Saturday. I hope you <u>will</u> forgive me.
Say: Underline all the auxiliary verbs and circle the progressive verb form.

Pupil book answers

Verbs: auxiliary verbs

Remember

Verbs have two **tenses**: past and present. Other **verb forms** are made by putting 'helper' verbs before the main verb. These helper verbs are called **auxiliary verbs**.

United <u>have been</u> woeful recently.   (perfect form)

Johnson <u>was waiting</u> at the far post.   (progressive form)

United <u>will face</u> City in the next round.   (future time)

Try it

1 Add the **auxiliary verb** needed to complete each sentence.

The girl _____was_____ fidgeting in her seat all through the show.

We _____have_____ chosen a name for our new puppy.

Dominic _____has_____ known Becky for years.

There _____will_____ be a full moon tonight.

It is late but the children _____are_____ still searching for the lost tortoise.

I _____do_____ not want gravy on my broccoli.

2 Rewrite each sentence using the **auxiliary verb** shown in brackets.

He explained it all to me.	He has explained it all to me.	(has)
I wrote a story about you.	I have written a story about you.	(have)
Her hands trembled.	Her hands were trembling.	(were)
I listen to the music.	I am listening to the music.	(am)
They are singing here today.	They will sing here today.	(will)
I like tea but not coffee.	I like tea but I do not like coffee.	(do)

Sentence practice

Write <u>two</u> different sentences using the verb 'beat' with the **auxiliary verb** 'have/has'.

United have beaten us three times already this season.

After you have beaten the egg, pour it into the pan.

10

Accept other auxiliary verbs if they make grammatical sense – for example, the modal verb 'might' in place of 'will', or 'had' in place of 'have'/'has'. However, 'are' must be used in the fifth sentence to maintain tense consistency.

[Note: Modal verbs are the focus of Lesson 18. The past perfect form using 'had' is covered in the next lesson, Lesson 8.]

Check that the pupils have made appropriate changes to the main verb [e.g. 'have written' not 'have wrote'].

Accept other grammatically correct alternatives [e.g. They will be singing here today. I do like tea but not coffee.].

These are just examples of sentences using the given main verb and auxiliary verb.

Compare the pupils' sentences. Discuss how they have used the perfect form to refer to recent events or those continuing into the present.

Lesson 8 Verbs: perfect forms

> Focus using present and past perfect verb forms to mark relationships of time and cause
>
> Key terms verb, perfect form, auxiliary verb, **present perfect**, **past perfect**
>
> Focus text Joe Bromley <u>is</u> now a rich man but he <u>has known</u> hard times.
> He <u>has become</u> a successful businessman but he <u>has not forgotten</u>
> his humble beginnings.
> Once Joe <u>had learnt</u> to drive, he <u>got</u> a job in Manchester.
> After a few years, the business <u>had grown</u> and he <u>was promoted</u>.

TEACH

Read aloud the first two sentences of the focus text and discuss what they tell us about Joe's life.

Discuss the verb forms used to refer to events in the past [he <u>has known</u>; he <u>has become</u>; he <u>has not forgotten</u>]. Remind the pupils that these are examples of the perfect verb form. This uses the auxiliary verb 'has'/'have'. Discuss why this verb form has been used [e.g. because events in the past are still ongoing or relevant now – Joe became successful and still is, he knew hard times and remembers them now].

Remind the pupils that some verbs change depending on whether we are using the simple past tense or the perfect tense [e.g. I knew/I have known; I forgot/I have forgotten].

Show the rest of the focus text to read about the events earlier in Joe's life. Discuss the order in which they happened and how one event led to another. Explain that each of these sentences tells us about two events that happened in the past. To show that one event happened earlier and resulted in the other, the past perfect form of the verb is used [e.g. Joe <u>had learnt</u> to drive – and so he got a job; the business <u>had grown</u> – and so Joe was promoted]. The past perfect form uses the auxiliary verb 'had' before the main verb.

[Note: In **Grammar 3** and **4**, the present perfect form was referred to simply as 'the perfect form'. You should now explain that the verb form that uses 'has'/'have' is called the *present* perfect form, whereas the verb form that uses 'had' is called the *past* perfect form.]

EXTEND Discuss other irregular verbs that take a different form in the perfect tense [e.g. rode/ridden].

PRACTISE

Pupil book page 11

APPLY

- The pupils use perfect forms when writing accounts, news reports or biographies in the past tense, to show the time relationship between events [e.g. There had been …].
- In stories, the pupils use perfect forms to refer back to significant events that had happened earlier [e.g. Once, he had been a rich man, but now …].
- The pupils use perfect forms when writing story summaries [e.g. X has gone missing …; X has found …].
- The pupils write an opening sentence for a story using a past perfect form [e.g. Jed had always been afraid of …]. They write a closing sentence to reflect on events [e.g. It had been an adventure.].
- In history, the pupils use past perfect forms to show time relationships and to refer back to events that took place earlier [e.g. The Romans had invaded …].

ASSESS

Dictation: The police arrived quickly but the thieves <u>had gone</u>. Police later found the car that the thieves <u>had abandoned</u> by the canal.
Say: Underline all the past perfect verb forms.

Pupil book answers

Verbs: perfect forms

Remember

The **present perfect form** uses the auxiliary verb 'has' or 'have' before the main verb. It is used to write about events that have happened in the recent past, are still ongoing or have consequences now. The **past perfect form** uses the auxiliary verb 'had' to show that one event happened before another past event.

Joe <u>has become</u> a successful businessman.   (present perfect)
Once Joe <u>had learnt</u> to drive, he got a job.   (past perfect)

Try it

1 Underline the **past perfect form** of verbs in these sentences.

The farmer <u>had been</u> outside chopping wood before he began to build the fire.

Once Dalia <u>had finished</u> her chores, she sat down for a rest.

The coach was pleased because the players <u>had done</u> their best.

I wanted to see Miss Braithwaite but she <u>had gone</u> for lunch.

Amber stared at the boy because she was sure she <u>had seen</u> him before.

Charlie was excited because he <u>had wanted</u> to visit Japan for a long time.

2 Rewrite each sentence using the **present perfect verb form** rather than the simple past tense.

The house <u>was</u> empty for months.   The house has been empty for months.

I <u>forgot</u> my password.   I have forgotten my password.

Rewrite each sentence using the **past perfect verb form** rather than the simple past tense.

I <u>finished</u> all my homework.   I had finished all my homework.

He <u>gave</u> away all his money.   He had given away all his money.

Sentence practice

Add <u>two</u> sentences about what had happened, using **past perfect verb forms**.

Kyle sat down and cried. It had been a disastrous day. At breakfast, he had

dropped the eggs on the floor. Then he had missed the bus.

11

Check that the pupils use the correct form of the main verb with 'has'/'have' [e.g. 'have forgotten', not 'have forgot'].

Discuss the effect of using the present perfect rather than the simple past tense [e.g. 'I have forgotten my password' suggests that it is still forgotten].

Check that the pupils use the correct form of the main verb with 'had' [e.g. 'had given', not 'had gave'].

Discuss the effect of using the past perfect rather than the simple past tense.

These are just examples of possible sentences using past perfect forms. Again, check that the pupils use the correct form of the main verb with 'had'.

Discuss why the past perfect works well here [e.g. to refer back to earlier events that explain why he sat down and cried].

Lesson 9 Standard English

Focus using Standard English verb forms and pronouns [I/me, them/those, that/what]

Key terms Standard English, non-Standard English, verb, pronoun

Focus text I asked George about when he first started to play sport. "Sport has always bin an important part of me life. Me brother and me was always playing footie in the park. Them was great days. The fun what we had."

TEACH

Show the focus text and read it aloud. Discuss how we can tell that the interviewer has written down George's words exactly as spoken [e.g. the inverted commas; the use of non-Standard English]. Ask the pupils to identify examples of non-Standard verbs. Underline them [bin, was].

Remind the pupils that although non-Standard verb forms are sometimes used in speech, in writing we should nearly always use Standard English verb forms. Work with the pupils to change the non-Standard verbs in the focus text to the Standard English forms [been, were].

Ask the pupils if they notice anything else that is not Standard English in George's first sentence ['me life' should be 'my life']. Explain that 'me' is a pronoun referring to myself, whereas 'my' is the determiner needed before the noun ['life'].

Ask the pupils if they notice any other non-standard use of pronouns in the focus text. For example, in George's second sentence, it should be 'My brother and I were always playing ...'. Explain that in Standard English, we use 'I' if it is *before* the verb, and 'me' if it comes *after* the verb [e.g. They played football with my brother and me.]. In the third sentence, it should be 'those were great days' rather than 'them were'. In the fourth sentence, it should be 'the fun that we had' rather than 'what we had'. [Note: The pupils will learn more about relative pronouns such as 'that' in Lesson 13.]

EXTEND Discuss other examples of non-Standard and informal language [e.g. footie].

PRACTISE

Pupil book page 12

APPLY

- The pupils write an interview, deliberately using non-Standard words and verb forms in the interviewee's responses to questions. They then rewrite the answers using Standard English.
- As part of a history project, the pupils interview local people. They try to write down what they say as they say it, including any non-Standard words or forms.
- The pupils write personal accounts or diaries, checking that the words 'I' and 'me' are used appropriately.
- When they are editing work, encourage the pupils to read sentences aloud, checking that Standard English is used [e.g. in verb forms and pronouns].

ASSESS

Dictation: Ethel and me worked in the kitchen. It were hard work. The washing up made me hands sore. There was none of them modern dishwashers in them days.
Say: Underline any words that are non-Standard English and write the Standard English words instead.
Answer: I, was, my, were, those, those

Pupil book answers

Standard English

Remember

Non-Standard English is sometimes used in speech, but in writing you should nearly always use Standard English. Pay attention to pronouns and verb forms, as these are often confused.

Sam and me was always playing in the park.
Them was great days.   (non-Standard English)
Sam and I were always playing in the park.
Those were great days.   (Standard English)

Try it

1 Add the correct word to complete each sentence using **Standard English**.

On Friday morning, Joseph and _____I_____ tidied the art cupboard.   (me I)

We decided to stack _____those_____ boxes on top of each other.   (them those)

It was a funny story _____that_____ he told us.   (what that)

I need _____my_____ glasses to read the newspaper.   (my me)

Mrs Hawkins sent Jude and _____me_____ to fetch the register.   (me I)

There is a lot of wildlife living in _____those_____ woods.   (them those)

2 Rewrite each sentence using **Standard English**.

Me and me dad have writ to the council about them bins left outside our house.
Dad and I have written to the council about those bins left outside our house.

I think them computer games what you wanted is in me bedroom.
I think those computer games that you wanted are in my bedroom.

It were so windy that it blowed me hat off me head and into them bushes over there.
It was so windy that it blew my hat off my head and into those bushes over there.

Sentence practice

Write a sentence using **non-Standard English**. Then rewrite it using Standard English.

Mum and me thought me brother were funny in the play.
Mum and I thought my brother was funny in the play.

These sentences also include examples of non-Standard verb forms that have been covered in previous books. Check that the correct forms have been used.

12

These are just examples of sentences illustrating non-Standard and Standard English. The sentences could include non-Standard verb forms and pronouns.

Lesson 10 Standard English: double negatives

Focus recognising and correcting double negatives in sentences

Key terms statement, Standard English, non-Standard English, **double negative**

Focus text **Officer:** Come on, Bill. You know something.
Bill: I told ya. I don't know nothing about it.
Officer: You saw somebody, didn't you?
Bill: I didn't see nobody.

TEACH

Show the focus text. Read it aloud using appropriate voices. Discuss the situation and the use of non-Standard English to represent natural speech [e.g. I told ya]. Discuss whether Bill is being a helpful witness [no – he is denying everything; he says he saw nothing].

Ask the pupils to identify Bill's two negative statements. Remind the pupils that negative statements use negative words such as 'no', 'nothing', 'never', 'nowhere' and 'not' [or the contraction –n't]. Underline the negative words used in the focus text. Point out that there are two negative words in each sentence [don't … nothing; didn't … nobody]. Ask: What is Bill really saying here? Is this the meaning he intended?

Explain that sometimes in speech people use two negative words in a sentence, as Bill does. This is called a double negative. Two negative words in one sentence cancel each other out, so the meaning is reversed and the sentence means the opposite of what was intended [e.g. 'I didn't see nobody' actually means that he did see someone]. Explain that double negatives are a problem because they leave the meaning unclear.

As well as being confusing, double negatives are also non-Standard English. For this reason, double negatives should be avoided when writing. Discuss how to change Bill's statements into Standard English so that there is only one negative word and the meaning is clear [I don't know anything about it./I know nothing about it. I didn't see anybody./I saw nobody.].

Ask the pupils to invent some more denials for Bill, using double negatives and then correcting them [e.g. I don't want to get into no trouble./I don't want to get into any trouble.].

EXTEND Discuss other non-Standard forms like 'I told ya' [e.g. a lotta/a lot of; 'cos/because].

PRACTISE

Pupil book page 13

APPLY

- The pupils write their own dialogue between two characters, making use of double negatives for a humorous effect [e.g. a young child denying responsibility for some unfortunate event].
- The pupils use negative sentences in factual texts [e.g. Some animals do not like …; They are never …].
- The pupils use negative statements in instructional texts to give warnings [e.g. Do not overheat.].
- Encourage the pupils to proofread all texts, checking for double negatives and rewording as necessary.

ASSESS

Dictation: My mum <u>never</u> throws <u>nothing</u> away. She won't let us throw any of our clothes away. She says we <u>can't</u> have <u>no</u> new ones until the old ones are completely worn out.
Say: Underline the double negatives.
Check: Both parts of the double negatives are underlined.

Pupil book answers

Standard English: double negatives

Remember

Negative words, including 'no', 'nothing', 'never' and 'not' (also written as the contraction –n't), are used in negative sentences. You only need <u>one</u> negative word in a sentence. If you use two negative words, they cancel each other out and the sentence means the opposite of what was intended.

I didn't see nobody.   ✗   (double negative)

I didn't see anybody. or I saw nobody.   ✓   (Standard English)

Try it

1 Add the correct word to complete each sentence using **Standard English.**

Max never told ___anybody___ about the argument.   (anybody nobody)

You're not going ___anywhere___ until you've finished. (nowhere anywhere)

I've never seen ___anything___ like it before.   (anything nothing)

Vasanth didn't have ___any___ brothers or sisters.   (no any)

I'm not going to play tennis ___ever___ again.   (never ever)

Jenny couldn't find ___any___ work at the factory.   (no any)

2 Rewrite these sentences so that the meaning is clear.

I don't want no sugar in my tea.   I don't want any sugar in my tea.

I'm not going nowhere this morning.   I'm not going anywhere this morning.

I don't know nothing about computers. I don't know anything about computers.

Holly's not talking to nobody today.   Holly's not talking to anybody today.

I never saw no lorry outside.   I never saw any lorry outside.

I don't trust none of them.   I don't trust any of them.

> There are other ways of constructing these sentences but there should only be one negative word.

Sentence practice

Write <u>three</u> sentences using **negative** words to give warnings. Remember to avoid double negatives.

Never cross a road without looking both ways.

Do not try to feed any of the animals in the zoo.

Leave nothing on the bus when you get off.

13

These are just examples of sentences using negative words to give warnings. Compare the pupils' answers.

Revision 1 answers

This page revises punctuation from **Grammar 3** and **4**. The pupils should be using this punctuation in their writing.

The focus of each activity is given in case further revision is needed.

Grammar 5   Schofield & Sims **Grammar and Punctuation**

Focus: commas to separate items in lists

In these sentences the list of items is placed before the main verb. You could discuss this sentence structure with the pupils.

There should be no comma before 'and'.

Focus: apostrophes to mark singular and plural possession

If the pupils are struggling, remind them to check the word *before* the apostrophe – it should be the owner or owners [a giraffe, the ants, the children, the invaders].

Focus: question tags; apostrophes in contracted forms; commas

This question checks the pupils' understanding of question tags. It also checks the use of apostrophes in –n't, and commas to separate the statement and question tag.

Revision 1

1 Insert **commas** in the correct places in these sentences.

Butterflies, dragonflies, mosquitoes, gnats and moths are all examples of flying insects.

A spacious living room, modern kitchen and large dining room can all be found on the ground floor.

Ripe mangoes, figs, sweet potatoes, colourful fabrics and shiny trinkets were just some of the things on sale at the market.

Mowing the lawn, raking up the leaves and planting the bulbs are some of the jobs I must do in the garden this weekend.

2 Rewrite the phrases below using an **apostrophe** to show **possession**.

the neck of a giraffe	a giraffe's neck
the nest belonging to the ants	the ants' nest
the playground for children	the children's playground
the settlement of the invaders	the invaders' settlement

3 Add a **question tag** to make each statement into a question. Punctuate it correctly.

It's Monday today , isn't it?

Mel likes strawberries , doesn't she?

We should wait for Owen , shouldn't we?

You collect football programmes , don't you?

4 One word in the sentence below uses an **apostrophe** incorrectly. Underline the word.

Mrs Neil's pupils stacked their chair's by the classroom door.

Explain why it is incorrect.

The 's' on 'chairs' is a plural 's', not 'apostrophe s' to show possession.

Focus: distinguishing plural –s and possessive –'s

The explanation should refer to the fact that 'chairs' is a plural noun, rather than a possessive.

Using an apostrophe with plural –s is a common error. Remind the pupils to check their own writing for errors like this when proofreading.

This page revises grammatical terms introduced in **Grammar 3** and **4** that the pupils should be familiar with.

The focus of each activity is given in case further revision is needed.

Schofield & Sims **Grammar and Punctuation**   Grammar 5

5 Use a different **co-ordinating conjunction** to add another **clause** to each sentence below.

Robbie's alarm clock began to bleep

but he did not wake up.

Robbie's mum always had to shake him

or he would never get up.

Robbie turned his pillow over

and he went back to sleep.

6 Complete each sentence with a different **possessive pronoun**.

This is _mine._

That is _yours._

These are _ours._

Those are _hers._

7 Rewrite the sentence below by moving an **adverbial** to the start of the sentence. Punctuate the new sentence correctly.

I sat down and replied to her letter immediately after lunch.

Immediately after lunch, I sat down and replied to her letter.

8 Underline the **main clause** in each sentence.

<u>There was a crash</u> as the man fell over.

Once Leo had found the address, <u>he set off down the road.</u>

<u>Nikesh crossed the track</u> so that he could read the sign.

Just as Bethany was about to step out of the front door, <u>she heard a strange noise.</u>

9 Rewrite the sentence below, adding a **subordinate clause**.

The people screamed.

The people screamed whenever the ground began to shake.

10 Label the boxes to show the **word class** each word belongs to.

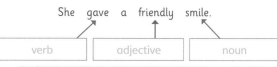

She   gave   a   friendly   smile.

| verb | adjective | noun |

15

Focus: co-ordinating conjunctions

These are just examples. Accept any grammatically correct sentences using, 'and', 'but' and 'or'. Check that the pupils do not use a subordinating conjunction [e.g. when; because].

Focus: possessive pronouns

Accept other possessive pronouns [e.g. his; theirs] as long as they are spelt correctly with no apostrophe.

Possessive determiners should not be used [e.g. not 'This is <u>my</u> book.'].

Focus: commas after fronted adverbials

Also accept: 'After lunch, I sat down and replied to her letter immediately.'

Focus: distinguishing main clauses from subordinate clauses

Remind the pupils that a main clause makes sense by itself.

Focus: recognising word classes

Check that the pupils do not label 'friendly' as an adverb just because it ends with –ly.

Focus: subordinate clauses

Any grammatically correct sentence with a subordinate clause and the correct punctuation is acceptable. If the subordinate clause is added at the start of the sentence, it should be followed by a comma.

Check that the pupils have not added a prepositional phrase [e.g. in the street] or a main clause [e.g. and they ran away].

Writing task 1: Analysis sheet

Tick the circles to show amount of evidence found in writing:

1 No evidence
2 Some evidence
3 Clear evidence

Pupil name: _____

Date: _____

Assessing punctuation

The writing sample demonstrates:	Evidence		
sentence boundaries demarcated with capital letters and appropriate end punctuation.	①	②	③
capital letters used for 'I' and proper nouns.	①	②	③
commas used to separate items in a list [e.g. names; short phrases].	①	②	③
apostrophes used correctly in contractions [e.g. don't] and for possession [e.g. Lucy's voice].	①	②	③
commas after fronted adverbials and before question tags.	①	②	③
direct speech punctuated correctly, including when spoken words are split.	①	②	③

Assessing grammar and sentence structure

The writing sample demonstrates:	Evidence		
grammatically correct sentences that use Standard English [e.g. verbs; agreement; pronouns].	①	②	③
sentence variation [e.g. short sentences; questions; exclamations used for effect].	①	②	③
expanded noun phrases to describe, specify and add detail.	①	②	③
adverbials to add detail and to vary sentence openings.	①	②	③
subordinate clauses, using a wide range of conjunctions to link clauses or ideas.	①	②	③
pronouns used to avoid repetition and aid cohesion, with no ambiguity.	①	②	③
varied use of verb forms to express time [e.g. progressive forms; perfect forms].	①	②	③

Key target: _____

Writing task 1: Pupil checklist

Name: _____   Date: _____

Reread what you have written to check that it makes sense. Tick the circle if you have correctly used the punctuation or grammar feature in your writing.

Punctuation

◯ I have used capital letters at the beginning of sentences, and full stops, question marks or exclamation marks at the end of sentences.

◯ I have used capital letters for 'I' and proper nouns.

◯ I have used commas to separate items in a list.

◯ I have used apostrophes in contractions (e.g. don't) and for possession (e.g. Lucy's voice).

◯ I have used commas after fronted adverbials and before question tags.

◯ I have used inverted commas and other punctuation in direct speech.

Grammar and sentences

◯ I have used grammatically correct sentences and Standard English.

◯ I have used varied sentence openings (e.g. fronted adverbials).

◯ I have used different sentence types (e.g. question, exclamation).

◯ I have used longer noun phrases to describe and give details.

◯ I have used adverbials to add detail about where, when, how and why.

◯ I have used sentences with subordinate clauses and a range of conjunctions.

◯ I have used pronouns rather than repeating nouns, and it is clear who or what the pronouns refer to.

◯ I have used different verb forms to express past time with some progressive and perfect forms.

Teacher feedback

My key target: _____

_____

Lesson 11 Determiners

Focus using a range of determiners to specify known or unknown nouns

Key terms noun, noun phrase, determiner

Focus text The report shows that many children travel to their local primary school in a car.
This school is introducing two new schemes to encourage our pupils to walk to school.
Some parents will be helping us to set up these schemes.

TEACH

Show the focus text and read it aloud. Discuss the issue raised, what type of text it might be and clues that suggest this [e.g. a letter from a school informing parents of a new scheme – 'this school', 'our pupils'; possibly persuading them that it is a good idea – 'the report shows'].

Ask the pupils what kind of words and phrases are underlined [nouns, noun phrases]. Can they remember the term used for the word before the noun, at the start of a noun phrase? [determiner] Invite the pupils to identify the determiners in the focus text [the, many, their, a, this, two, our, some, these], and circle them.

Explain that a range of words can be used as determiners. [Note: Determiners can be grouped into various categories, including articles, but the pupils are not required to know the different types.] Remind the pupils that some determiners can also be used in different ways. For example, 'this', 'these' and 'some' can also be used as pronouns. However, if they are used before a noun they are determiners. [Note: Pronoun/ determiner confusions are covered in more detail in Lesson 27.]

Discuss the function of determiners – how they are used to 'determine' or specify the noun as known or unknown. For example, in 'the report', 'this school', 'our pupils', all the determiners refer to a specific known noun. In other phrases, the determiner refers to the noun in general [e.g. a car], or an unknown noun [e.g. some parents].

Invite the pupils to change the determiner before a noun and discuss how this changes the meaning [e.g. this school/your school/Bill's school/one school/a school/every school/all schools].

EXTEND Discuss and classify the different types of determiner. These include articles [the, a/an]; possessives [e.g. their; our; its]; demonstratives [e.g. this; these]; numbers [e.g. two] and quantifiers [e.g. some; many].

PRACTISE

Pupil book page 18

APPLY

- When writing reports, the pupils use determiners to start with general statements [e.g. Some metals ...; Most metals ...] and then move to specific statements [e.g. Two soft metals ...].
- The pupils write personal accounts using determiners to specify known nouns [e.g. my dog].
- The pupils write instructions using a range of determiners to specify nouns [e.g. six spoonfuls; both tins].

ASSESS

Dictation: In the fridge, she found some water, two jars of jam and an empty bottle of milk. There was no bread. "I can't just eat that jam," she said to herself.
Say: Underline all the determiners.
Check: Commas are used correctly and the direct speech is correctly punctuated.

Pupil book answers

Determiners

Remember

A **determiner** is the word that comes before a **noun** or at the start of a noun phrase. Many different types of words can be used as determiners. They can tell you whether the noun is known or unknown.

| the report | this school | our pupils | two schemes | (known) |
| a car | an idea | some parents | many children | (unknown) |

Try it

1 Underline all the **determiners** in each sentence.

<u>Some</u> new houses are cramped but <u>this</u> house has <u>a</u> spacious living room.

<u>Every</u> magnet has <u>two</u> poles, <u>a</u> north pole and <u>a</u> south pole.

<u>The</u> room was small, with <u>one</u> window overlooking <u>her</u> little garden.

<u>Most</u> lizards have <u>four</u> legs but some, such as <u>the</u> slow-worm, have <u>no</u> legs.

<u>All</u> bats in <u>this</u> country are protected by <u>the</u> law.

It took <u>many</u> weeks and <u>much</u> effort for <u>those</u> brave explorers to reach <u>the</u> North Pole.

2 Complete each sentence using suitable **determiners**.

_____Most_____ metals are hard but _____some_____ metals are softer and more flexible.

_____A_____ mole uses _____its_____ front feet to loosen _____the_____ earth when it is digging.

Behind us, there was _____an_____ empty space with _____two_____ trees in the middle but _____no_____ grass.

_____Those_____ seagulls just swooped down for _____some_____ crumbs left from _____our_____ sandwiches.

_____Some_____ animals such as _____the_____ chameleon can change _____their_____ colour to match _____the_____ background.

Sentence practice

Write a sentence about a puppy, using <u>three</u> different **determiners**.

That puppy you found in your garden is our Yorkshire terrier.

This activity includes a range of words used as determiners. Remind the pupils that a determiner comes before a noun. Sometimes an adjective comes between the determiner and the noun [e.g. some <u>new</u> houses].

In the fourth sentence, the word 'some' should not be underlined as it is used as a pronoun in place of a noun, rather than a determiner before a noun.

Other determiners will work in some of these sentences [e.g. A mole uses both front feet ...].

Compare and discuss the pupils' answers, discussing appropriate choices [e.g. 'a mole' to make a generalised statement; 'our sandwiches' to specify known objects].

Check for the correct use of 'a'/'an' if used [e.g. A mole; an empty space].

This is just an example. Any sentence is acceptable if it uses three different determiners. In this sentence, the determiners are used to specify the nouns as known.

Lesson 12   Expanded noun phrases

> Focus   using noun phrases to convey information concisely
>
> Key terms   noun, noun phrase, determiner, adjective, prepositional phrase
>
> Focus text   Almost all squirrels in this area are grey squirrels. They have dense silvery grey fur with a brown tinge along the back. They have a bushy, grey tail and ears without tufts.
> They are tree squirrels. Their long, muscular hind legs and short front legs help them to leap. Sharp claws are used for gripping bark and the long tail helps them to balance.

TEACH

Show the focus text and read it aloud. Discuss what it tells us about squirrels [e.g. what sort of squirrels live in the area; what they look like; how they are adapted to life in trees].

Explain that some of the key words in the text are highlighted. These are nouns – for example, naming parts of the squirrel [e.g. fur; tail; ears; legs]. Built around these nouns are longer noun phrases that describe or specify the noun. Ask the pupils to find examples of longer [or expanded] noun phrases in the focus text. Underline the noun phrases and discuss why the nouns were expanded [e.g. to specify *which* squirrels – 'all squirrels in this area', 'grey squirrels'; to add important information or descriptive detail].

Discuss the underlined phrases, identifying the different types of word used to modify the nouns [e.g. determiners – '<u>all</u> squirrels'; adjectives – '<u>bushy</u>, <u>grey</u> tail'; prepositional phrases added after the noun – 'ears <u>without tufts</u>']. Point out that where another noun is used, such as in '<u>tree</u> squirrel', it specifies the noun – in this case, the type of squirrel: one that lives in trees.

Explain that expanded noun phrases like those in the focus text help to convey relevant information in a concise way – for example, when describing the squirrel's fur [They have <u>dense silvery grey fur with a brown tinge along the back</u>.]. The extra detail provided by the adjectives and prepositional phrases helps to describe the quality and variation in colour of the squirrel's fur.

EXTEND   Discuss the use of adverbs to expand noun phrases [e.g. a <u>slightly</u> larger tail].

PRACTISE

Pupil book page 19

APPLY

- In explanations, reports or other non-fiction writing, the pupils use factual and precise nouns and noun phrases [e.g. tropical regions; many violent explosions; a small rounded snout].
- The pupils write 'wanted' posters, using expanded noun phrases to describe characters from stories [e.g. a large, stocky man with a limp].
- The pupils use concise noun phrases when writing newspaper reports [e.g. two second-half goals from free kicks].
- Encourage the pupils to use a thesaurus to find adjectives to use in expanded noun phrases.

ASSESS

Dictation: In <u>a small wooden house by the shore of a lake</u>, there lived <u>a rich widow with three sons</u>. To the east of the lake, there stood <u>a great mountain with snow on the top</u>.
Say: Underline the noun phrases built around the words 'house', 'widow' and 'mountain'.
Check: The complete noun phrase is underlined, including determiners.

Pupil book answers

Expanded noun phrases

Remember

You can add words and phrases to **nouns** to form expanded **noun phrases**. These help to give more information about the noun. An expanded noun phrase might include a **determiner**, one or more **adjectives**, other nouns and/or **prepositional phrases**.

squirrel → the squirrel → the grey squirrel
→ the graceful grey squirrel → the graceful
grey tree squirrel with a long bushy tail

Try it

1 Underline the expanded **noun phrase** built around each **noun** in **bold**.

The biologist gave a very interesting **talk** about unusual animals.

A green grass **snake** with small black markings slithered into view.

We visited several interesting ancient **monuments** while on holiday in Italy.

Deer have branched **antlers** with a velvety covering.

From his balcony, he could look out over the golden **roofs** of the city.

I tried to count the glittering **stars** in the sapphire sky.

2 Rewrite each sentence using an expanded **noun phrase**.

We sell hats.   We sell extravagant hats for weddings and special occasions.

I came to a door.   I came to a bright blue door with a shiny brass knob in the middle.

Once there was a cat. Once there was an enchanted cat with fiery green eyes and beautiful black fur.

This is a butterfly. This is a magnificent butterfly from the tropical rainforests of Africa.

Sentence practice

Write a sentence about an elaborate feast. Use **three** expanded **noun phrases**.

On the table were silver plates with spicy morsels, steaming dishes of roasted partridge in pomegranate juice and towers of the finest exotic fruit from faraway lands.

Remind the pupils to underline the longest possible noun phrase, expanding before and after the noun. Check that the determiner is included.

These are just examples of how the nouns might be expanded to describe, specify or add detail. Look for interesting adjectives and expanding before and after the noun. Compare and discuss the pupils' answers.

You could discuss why the nouns might need to be expanded [e.g. to specify what sort of hats; to make the cat seem intriguing; to give information about the butterfly].

This is just an example of how expanded noun phrases might be used to create a picture of an elaborate feast in just a sentence. Encourage the use of interesting words, and perhaps invite the pupils to use a thesaurus when composing their sentences.

Compare and discuss the pupils' sentences to decide which are the most effective and why.

19

Lesson 13 Relative clauses 1

Focus introducing relative clauses beginning with relative pronouns [who, that, which, whose] or an omitted relative pronoun

Key terms **relative clause**, subordinate clause, **relative pronoun**, noun

Focus text Once, there was a king who had a threadbare cloak.
The crown that he wore was made of tin.
He had a wonky throne, which had a broken seat.
He was the only king whose castle was for sale.

TEACH

Show the focus text and read each sentence aloud. Ask: What makes this king rather unusual?

Discuss which parts of the sentence give the important details about the king, his crown and his throne. Underline the words that come after the noun [who had a threadbare cloak; that he wore; which had a broken seat; whose castle was for sale].

Explain that the underlined words are a special type of subordinate clause called a relative clause. Rather than giving extra information about a verb or an event, a relative clause tells us more about a noun, so the information relates to a person [e.g. the king] or a thing [e.g. his crown].

Relative clauses begin with a type of pronoun called a relative pronoun. Identify and circle the relative pronouns in the focus text [who, that, which, whose]. Explain that relative pronouns refer back to nouns already mentioned, so we do not need to repeat the noun [e.g. 'He had a wonky throne. The throne had a broken seat.' becomes 'He had a wonky throne, which had a broken seat.']. This is a neat way of clarifying the noun or adding important extra information about it.

Point out that we use the relative pronoun 'who' when referring to a person [the king] and the relative pronouns 'that' or 'which' when referring to things [e.g. the crown; the throne]. The relative pronoun 'whose' is used in place of a possessive word [e.g. the king's castle/his castle]. Explain that sometimes the relative pronoun can be left out and the sentence will still make sense [e.g. The crown that he wore was made of tin.]. [Note: This is also covered in Lesson 15 and in **Grammar 6**.]

Invite the pupils to form sentences following the same pattern [e.g. Once, there was a farmer who …].

EXTEND Explain that a comma is sometimes used to separate a relative clause from the main clause, as in the third sentence of the focus text. This is often done before the word 'which', or when non-vital information is added to the sentence. [Note: This is covered in **Grammar 6**.]

PRACTISE

Pupil book page 20

APPLY

- In stories, the pupils use relative clauses to add details about people and important objects.
- The pupils use relative clauses in non-fiction texts to define or clarify [e.g. A reptile is an animal that …].
- When they are editing writing, encourage the pupils to look for opportunities to use relative clauses to add detail to nouns or to avoid repetition of nouns.

ASSESS

Dictation: The house that we lived in was in James Street. Mum always liked to talk to the woman who lived across the road. She was the lady whose husband was in the army.
Say: Underline the relative clauses and circle the relative pronouns.
Check: The relative pronoun is included within each underlined clause.

Pupil book answers

Relative clauses 1

Remember

You can use a **relative clause** to give more information about a **noun** mentioned in a sentence. A relative clause usually begins with a **relative pronoun**, such as 'who', 'which', 'that' or 'whose'.

Once, there was a poor king <u>who had a threadbare cloak</u>.
The crown <u>that he wore</u> was made of tin.

In some relative clauses the relative pronoun is missed out.
The crown ~~that~~ <u>he wore</u> was made of tin.

Try it

1 Underline the **relative clause** in each sentence. Circle the **relative pronoun**.

Mum has a friend (who) works at the hospital.

She came to the old brick wall, (which) ran round the side of the house.

The fish had silver scales (that) glittered red and gold.

The robins (that) we see in the garden are quite tame.

We spoke to the man (whose) house was struck by lightning.

We would like to thank everyone (who) helped us with our bake sale.

2 Complete each **relative clause** to give information about the **noun**.

I sent an email to my friend who lives in America.

She climbed down the rope that was hanging out of the window.

I met an old man whose name was Ernest Merriman.

I read the book, which explained everything.

He told us about his daughter who works in parliament.

She picked up the shovel that was lying on the ground.

Sentence practice

Write an interesting fact about a teacher, using a **relative clause**.

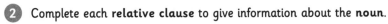

Mr Jackson is the teacher who taught me how to read.

20

Check that the pupils have correctly identified the relative clause in the fourth sentence, where it is in the middle of the sentence.

You could discuss what the relative clause adds to the sentence [e.g. specifying or making it clear which of Mum's friends it is].

These are just examples of how the pupils might complete the sentences. Compare their answers, discussing what information has been added.

Although the focus here is on adding important 'defining' information about the noun, the pupils may add additional non-essential information as well. This is acceptable for the moment as long as the sentence makes sense. [Note: Different types of relative clause are covered in **Grammar 6**.]

This is just an example of a suitable sentence using a relative clause to add more detail about which teacher it is.

Lesson 14 Relative clauses 2

Focus introducing relative clauses beginning with adverbs [where, when]

Key terms noun, relative clause, relative pronoun, adverb

Focus text We stayed in a house. The house was haunted.
We stayed in a house <u>that was haunted</u>.
At the end of the street, there was a house. No-one ever went to the house.
At the end of the street, there was a house <u>where no-one ever went</u>.

TEACH

Show the first part of the focus text. Read the two separate sentences and then the single sentence that combines the two pieces of information. Discuss how the single sentence is neater and more concise. Ask the pupils to name the part of the sentence that is underlined [relative clause – beginning with the relative pronoun 'that']. Remind the pupils that relative clauses give more information relating to a noun [e.g. here specifying which house they stayed in].

Show the second set of sentences. Again, read and compare the two separate sentences with the single sentence. Discuss how the single sentence combines the information and is more effective [e.g. it is more concise; it does not repeat the noun 'house'].

Explain that the underlined part of the sentence is again a relative clause. It tells us more about the house, distinguishing it from other houses. Explain that some relative clauses start with the words 'where' or 'when'. We use 'where' to refer to places and 'when' to refer to time [e.g. Today is the day <u>when</u> we move into the house.].

Invite the pupils to orally compose other sentences based on the ones in the focus text [e.g. At the end of the world, there is a land where …].

EXTEND Experiment with using the relative clause in different positions [e.g. The house <u>where I was born</u> is in Bury.].

PRACTISE

Pupil book page 21

APPLY

• The pupils construct sentences for a tourist brochure, using relative clauses to give information about the place [e.g. Wigan is the place where …].
• The pupils write imaginative sentences using relative clauses [e.g. Today is the day when all your dreams come true.].
• When they are writing, encourage the pupils to orally compose sentences, using relative clauses to combine information from two sentences or to add more information about a noun.
• The pupils use relative clauses in stories to add detail about places [e.g. a land where …; the house where …].

ASSESS

Dictation: Come with me to a faraway land where the sun never sets. This is the land where purple trees grow along flowing yellow rivers.
Say: Add another sentence using a relative clause to give more detail about this imaginary place.
Answer: e.g. This is a land where it never rains.

Pupil book answers

Relative clauses 2

Remember

A **relative clause** tells you more about a **noun**. Some relative clauses begin with 'where' or 'when'. You use 'where' to refer to places and 'when' to refer to times.

At the end of the street, there was a house where no-one ever went.

Try it

1 Use the words 'where' or 'when' to complete the **relative clause** in each sentence.

It was a long walk back to the caravan park ____where____ we were staying.

1969 was the year ____when____ man first landed on the moon.

We go swimming at the leisure centre ____where____ my mother works.

Today is the day ____when____ our cousins arrive back from Greece.

March is the month ____when____ the daffodils start to grow in my aunt's garden.

Visit the town of Stratford-upon-Avon ____where____ Shakespeare was born.

You may wish to point out that the second, fourth and fifth sentences could be written without the adverb 'when', in the same way that relative pronouns can sometimes be omitted from sentences.

2 Rewrite each sentence using a **relative clause** to add the information shown in brackets.

It was Monday afternoon.   (The hurricane struck on Monday afternoon.)

It was Monday afternoon when the hurricane struck.

This is New Street Station.   (We catch the train to London from New Street Station.)

This is New Street Station where we catch the train to London.

There is still a stain on the carpet.   (Dad dropped a tin of paint on the carpet.)

There is still a stain on the carpet where Dad dropped a tin of paint.

You could discuss how using a relative clause helps to give the information more concisely [e.g. by avoiding repetition].

Sentence practice

Complete this sentence using a **relative clause**.

I remember the day when I started school.

21

This is an example of a suitable sentence. You could ask the pupils to orally construct a number of sentences using this sentence stem and then choose one to record.

Lesson 15   Parenthesis: brackets

Focus   using brackets to indicate parenthesis

Key terms   **brackets, parenthesis**

Focus text   Jesse Owens (1913–1980) won four gold medals at the 1936 Olympics.

Jesse Owens (an American athlete) won four gold medals at the 1936 Olympics.

Jesse Owens (my dad's sporting hero) won four gold medals at the 1936 Olympics.

TEACH

Show the first sentence of the focus text. Read it aloud using appropriate intonation for the part in brackets. Discuss what it tells us and what sort of text it might come from [e.g. biography; encyclopedia].

Discuss the purpose of the information in the brackets [it tells us more about Jesse Owens]. Reveal the other sentences and discuss what extra information they provide [e.g. factual detail; a comment from the author].

Explain that when we add extra information into a sentence like this it is called a parenthesis. A parenthesis is not essential to the meaning of the sentence. Each sentence in the focus text still makes sense if we remove the parenthesis. Using parenthesis is a useful way of adding extra information or detail into a sentence.

Explain that brackets are used to clearly separate the parenthesis [the extra non-essential information] from the main sentence. A good way of checking that the brackets are in the right place is to read the rest of the sentence without the part in the brackets. The sentence should still make sense.

Point out that the parenthesis, or extra detail, can be a word, phrase or clause. Relative clauses can be added as a parenthesis, as in the focus text. Sometimes the relative pronoun is omitted [e.g. ~~who is~~ my dad's sporting hero]. [Note: This is covered in more detail in **Grammar 6**.]

Invite the pupils to compose some more sentences about Jesse Owens, using a parenthesis [e.g. Jesse Owens (an Olympic champion) was born in 1913.].

EXTEND   Discuss how commas could be used in place of the brackets. [Note: This is the focus of the next lesson, Lesson 16.]

PRACTISE

Pupil book page 22

APPLY

- The pupils write a biography of a famous person, using brackets to add dates and additional detail.
- The pupils write an informal letter or diary entry, using brackets to add comments and asides.
- When writing factual reports and explanations, the pupils use brackets to give additional information within a sentence rather than as a separate sentence.
- The pupils write a play script using brackets to add stage directions.

ASSESS

Dictation: Robert Louis Stevenson (1850–1894) wrote both stories and poems. His famous book Treasure Island (an exciting tale of pirates and villains) was first published in 1883.

Check: The brackets are correctly positioned. Capital letters are used for the proper nouns.

Pupil book answers

Parenthesis: brackets

Remember

Sometimes extra detail is added into a sentence. This may be something interesting but not essential to the sentence's meaning. You use <u>two</u> **brackets** to clearly separate the extra information (or **parenthesis**) from the main sentence.

Jesse Owens (<u>an American athlete</u>) won four gold medals at the 1936 Olympics.

Try it

1 Underline the extra information (**parenthesis**) that has been added in each sentence. Then insert the missing **brackets**.

Mrs Bahra (<u>our neighbour</u>) is always watching us from her window.

For breakfast, there was scrambled egg (<u>which I hate</u>) or porridge.

The tower (<u>built in 1853</u>) will soon be open to the public again.

The giant panda (<u>which lives in China</u>) is extremely rare.

Charles Dickens (<u>1812–1870</u>) was a famous and popular writer.

We spoke to Mr Cooper (<u>the school's head teacher</u>) about the building work.

2 Rewrite each sentence using **brackets** to add a **parenthesis** where shown by the arrow.

Grandma's dogs travel everywhere with her.

 Grandma's dogs (Trixie and Tinkerbell) travel everywhere with her.

Jack was the first to complete the puzzle.

Jack (who was the last to start) was the first to complete the puzzle.

This book is my favourite story of all time.

 This book (which is by Roald Dahl) is my favourite story of all time.

Sentence practice

Write <u>two</u> sentences about a member of your family. Use **brackets** to add a **parenthesis** to each sentence.

My brother Edward (sometimes called Eddie) wants to be an inventor. He makes

strange gadgets (which usually don't work) and spends hours drawing diagrams.

22

Remind the pupils to check that the brackets are in the correct place by reading the rest of the sentence without the part in the brackets – it should still make sense.

You may wish to discuss the use of relative clauses in parenthesis, perhaps identifying examples with pronouns and those with omitted pronouns [e.g. ~~who is~~ our neighbour; ~~which was~~ built in 1853].

These are examples of the sort of phrases or clauses that might be added as a parenthesis.

Check that the brackets are correctly positioned.

These are examples of the sort of sentences the pupils might write.

Check that the sentences are correctly punctuated, with the brackets correctly positioned around the parenthesis.

Lesson 16 Parenthesis: commas and dashes

> Focus using dashes or commas to indicate parenthesis
>
> Key terms parenthesis, brackets, comma, **dash**
>
> Focus text Jamie's mother, <u>who was a great cook</u>, had been baking all day. We went into the kitchen to find that the cakes – all ten of them – had vanished!

TEACH

Show the first sentence of the focus text and read it aloud. Discuss what two things it tells us about Jamie's mother and how this information is given. Ask the pupils what they notice about the part of the sentence that is underlined [e.g. it is a relative clause; it gives an extra detail about Jamie's mother that is not essential to the meaning of the main sentence].

Remind the pupils that adding a detail like this into a sentence is called using parenthesis. Explain that the writer could have put this information in brackets but has chosen to use two commas instead. It makes the parenthesis less obvious.

Show the second sentence in the focus text and read it aloud. Discuss what it tells us about the cakes. Ask the pupils to identify the parenthesis or extra information about the cakes that has been added into the sentence [all ten of them]. Ask what punctuation mark has been used to separate the parenthesis from the main sentence [two dashes]. Discuss how the two dashes make the parenthesis more obvious. Here it helps to create a more surprising effect.

Explain that we can use two commas or two dashes in the same way as we use brackets to separate a parenthesis from the main sentence. The same rules apply: place the first comma or dash before the start of the parenthesis and the second after the end. Use the focus text to show that we can ignore the part of the sentence between the commas or dashes and the rest of the sentence will still make sense.

Invite the pupils to orally compose other sentences based on these models [e.g. Aisha went into her classroom to find ...]. Use a curled finger to represent the comma and a straight hand to represent a dash.

EXTEND Discuss when we might use the different forms of punctuation [e.g. commas, which are smoother and more flowing, are often used in formal writing; dashes, which are more abrupt, are often used for effect, when we want to draw attention to the parenthesis].

PRACTISE

Pupil book page 23

APPLY

- The pupils write informal letters or diaries, using brackets and dashes to include asides, or comments to the reader, in parenthesis.
- The pupils write information texts or news reports, using commas to include extra details in parenthesis.
- The pupils write character descriptions, using parentheses marked by commas to drop in extra details that help to build up a picture of the character.
- In stories, the pupils construct sentences using a parenthesis to add in some surprising, dramatic or humorous extra details. They could use two dashes to draw attention and add to the effect.

ASSESS

Dictation: The note, scrawled in green ink, was on her desk. Maisie – quick as a flash – picked it up and put it in her pocket.
Say: Use commas in one of these sentences and dashes in the other.

Pupil book answers

Schofield & Sims **Grammar and Punctuation**   Grammar 5

Parenthesis: commas and dashes

Remember

You can use <u>two</u> **commas** or <u>two</u> **dashes** instead of brackets to show a **parenthesis** in a sentence. As with brackets, the dashes or commas clearly separate the extra information from the main sentence.

Jamie's mother, <u>who was a great cook</u>, had been baking all day. The cakes – <u>all ten of them</u> – had vanished!

Try it

1 Rewrite each sentence using **dashes** or **commas** to separate the extra information (the **parenthesis**) from the main sentence.

The Moon although it appears to be silver actually has no light.

The Moon, although it appears to be silver, actually has no light.

Jamila's father who is a doctor told us about his work at the hospital.

Jamila's father, who is a doctor, told us about his work at the hospital.

The water was cold really freezing so we quickly jumped out again.

The water was cold – really freezing – so we quickly jumped out again.

They threw everything bills, letters and notes into the bin.

They threw everything – bills, letters and notes – into the bin.

2 Add a **parenthesis** into the sentence. Use **commas** or **dashes** to punctuate it.

The city _____ – which was full of noise and colour – _____ was an exciting place to be.

Mars _____, the fourth planet of the Solar System, _____ is smaller than Earth.

Gavin _____ – rather surprisingly – _____ won the competition.

The casket _____, which is made of silver, _____ is now on display in the museum.

Sentence practice

Write a sentence about a messy ice cream, including a **parenthesis**. Use **commas** or **dashes** to punctuate it.

My ice cream – which was chocolate flavour – dripped all over my white T-shirt.

23

The pupils could use dashes rather than commas in the first and second sentences, but you may wish to discuss how commas tend to be more appropriate in formal, factual texts.

In the fourth sentence, you may wish to discuss how dashes are a better choice, as the parenthesis already includes a comma.

Remind the pupils to check that the punctuation is in the right place by reading the rest of the sentence to see that it makes sense.

These are just examples. Compare the pupils' answers.

Again, the pupils could use commas or dashes but you may wish to discuss when commas or dashes seem more appropriate and why.

This is just an example of a possible sentence using a parenthesis. The sentence could be punctuated with two commas or two dashes.

45

Lesson 17 Adverbs and possibility

Focus using adverbs to show different degrees of possibility [e.g. perhaps; surely]

Key terms adverb

Focus text **Dan:**   I think we should try to get out of here.
Ruby: I agree. That is definitely the best idea.
Sunita: Perhaps ... but maybe we should wait for help.
Alex: We clearly can't stay here. Obviously, Dan is right.

TEACH

Show the focus text. Read it aloud using appropriate intonation. Discuss what the situation might be [e.g. the characters are trapped or lost] and the characters' possible courses of action.

Discuss which of the characters seem most certain about Dan's idea [Ruby, Alex] and who sounds less certain and suggests another possibility [Sunita]. Discuss which words make the characters sound certain or less certain [the highlighted words]. Ask the pupils to name the type of word highlighted [adverbs].

The pupils will be familiar with adverbs that show manner, time and place, but the adverbs in the focus text have a different purpose. Explain that these adverbs show different levels of certainty and that we use them when discussing possibilities. Discuss which of the adverbs sound certain [definitely, clearly, obviously] and which sound less certain [perhaps, maybe].

Discuss how adverbs change the meaning of a sentence, using examples from the focus text [e.g. We should wait for help./Maybe, we should wait for help. We can't stay here./We clearly can't stay here.]. Ask: What do the adverbs add? [e.g. 'maybe' makes it sound like only a possibility; 'clearly' makes it sound certain]

Point out that sometimes the adverbs are used at the start of a sentence [Perhaps, ..., Obviously, ...], followed by a comma. Explain that adverbs are also used before or after the verb [is definitely, clearly can't]. Invite the pupils to experiment with moving some of the adverbs [e.g. Clearly, we can't stay here. Dan is obviously right.].

Discuss other adverbs that we can use to show possibility [e.g. possibly; probably] or certainty [e.g. surely; certainly]. Invite the pupils to use these to orally compose more sentences [e.g. Surely, help will come.].

EXTEND Challenge the pupils to use a thesaurus to find other examples [e.g. of course; undoubtedly].

PRACTISE

Pupil book page 24

APPLY

- In speech and writing, the pupils use adverbs showing certainty [e.g. surely; clearly; obviously] to help state an opinion or put a case forcefully.
- The pupils use adverbs of possibility when predicting events in stories, in group discussions or in reading journals [e.g. Perhaps, ...; Maybe, ...].
- In other subject areas, the pupils use adverbs of possibility to explore ideas and suggest possibilities [e.g. reasons for an event in history or a phenomenon in science].
- The pupils use adverbs of possibility to modify statements [e.g. I will need .../I will probably need ...].

ASSESS

Dictation: Should I enter the competition or not? I am certainly a good swimmer. I would definitely get to the final. Maybe, I would win it. It is probably too late to enter now.
Say: Underline the sentences where the adverbs show certainty.

Pupil book answers

Adverbs and possibility

Remember

Adverbs can be used when discussing possibilities. The adverbs can suggest different levels of certainty. Some adverbs make ideas sound certain, while others make them sound less sure.

That is definitely the best idea. We clearly can't stay here.　(certain)

Perhaps ... but maybe we should wait.　　　　　　　　(less certain)

Try it

1　Underline the **adverb** in each sentence. Then tick any sentences with adverbs that show certainty.

The bad weather <u>possibly</u> caused the accident. ☐

I will <u>certainly</u> arrive before the party ends. ☑

I think I could <u>probably</u> swim across the river. ☐

<u>Surely</u>, this will solve the problem. ☑

He was <u>obviously</u> the best singer in the competition. ☑

<u>Perhaps</u>, we will go on holiday in July. ☐

2　Rewrite each sentence using an **adverb** to make it sound more certain.

The new machine will work.　　The new machine will definitely work.

This answer is wrong.　　　　Obviously, this answer is wrong.

I think this is the best book.　I think this is clearly the best book.

Rewrite each sentence using an **adverb** to make it sound less certain.

We will win the lottery.　　　Maybe, we will win the lottery.

This will cheer you up.　　　Perhaps, this will cheer you up.

I could be there by two o'clock.　I could possibly be there by two o'clock.

The pupils could use other adverbs and/or use them in different positions [e.g. Surely, this answer is wrong. This answer is clearly wrong.].

If the adverb is used at the start of the sentence, then a comma should be added.

Sentence practice

Write <u>two</u> sentences about why a boy is waving at you, using **adverbs** to show different levels of possibility.

The boy clearly wants to catch my attention. Perhaps, he needs my help.

24

These are just examples of sentences the pupils might write giving possible reasons why the boy is waving. Look for sentences showing different levels of possibility – perhaps one with an adverb to sound certain [e.g. clearly; obviously] and one using an adverb to suggest a possibility [e.g. maybe; perhaps].

Lesson 18 Modal verbs and possibility

Focus using modal verbs to show different degrees of possibility

Key terms auxiliary verb, **modal verb**, adverb

Focus text Today will be a good day. I shall stay in bed until 10 o'clock.
Then I can have boiled eggs for breakfast. This afternoon I could
go swimming. Then I might watch a film this evening.

TEACH

Show the focus text and read it aloud. Discuss the plans for the day.

Ask the pupils which of the activities sound certain or most likely to happen [e.g. I shall stay in bed] and
which sound like possibilities or options – things the speaker *could* do [e.g. I could go swimming]. Discuss
which words show that these things are a possibility [e.g. could go; might watch].

Work with the pupils to underline the verbs in the focus text [e.g. will be; shall stay]. Explain that the verbs
are made up of a main verb and an auxiliary or 'helper' verb. Circle the auxiliary verbs [will, shall, can,
could, might]. Explain that these are called modal verbs. Modal verbs modify or change the meaning of
the main verbs to show different levels of possibility. We use them when expressing possibilities or future
happenings to show levels of certainty or how likely something is.

Discuss how the modal verbs affect the meaning of the sentences in the focus text – for example, which of
the modal verbs show certainty about the event [will, shall, can] and which show possibility [could, might].
Invite the pupils to swap the modal verbs in these sentences and discuss how this changes the meaning
[e.g. Today might be a good day. I will go swimming.]. Explain that modal verbs are useful in speech and
writing because they allow us to show these shades of meaning.

Explain that adverbs can be used alongside modal verbs to strengthen the effect [e.g. Clearly, today will
be a good day.]. Invite the pupils to add adverbs to the other sentences [e.g. I shall obviously stay in bed
...; Then I might possibly watch a film ...].

EXTEND Discuss the use of modal verbs in conditional sentences [e.g. If it's warm, I could go for a
picnic.]. [Note: Conditional sentences are covered in Lesson 30.]

PRACTISE

Pupil book page 25

APPLY

- The pupils write about an important issue [e.g. conservation], using modal verbs to refer to possibilities
or make predictions about the future [e.g. It could be ...; There might be a time when ...].
- When presenting an argument or point of view, the pupils use modal verbs to show certainty [e.g. We
must stop bullying in our school. We can ... We will ...].
- The pupils write about book characters or famous people, using modal verbs to speculate about how
their lives could have been different or might continue [e.g. She might have been ...; She could still ...].
- The pupils write horoscopes, using modal verbs to show possibilities [e.g. You will ...; You might ...].
- When they are editing writing, encourage the pupils to look for opportunities to use modal verbs.

ASSESS

Dictation: We are going to hold a cake sale. Mr Green says we can hold it in the hall. Miss Wilson might
help us with the cakes. It could be next week. We will make lots of money.
Say: Circle the modal verbs. Underline the sentences where the modal verbs show possibility.

Pupil book answers

Modal verbs and possibility

Remember

Modal verbs are used with other **verbs** to show different levels of possibility. They can make statements sound certain or more like a possibility.

Today will be a good day.   (certain)
This afternoon I could go swimming. (possible)

Try it

1 Underline the **modal verb** in each sentence. Write whether the modal verb makes it sound **certain** or **possible**.

We <u>can</u> get to the top of this mountain.   certain

This bridge <u>could</u> collapse at any moment.   possible

We <u>must</u> take some sun cream to the beach.   certain

There <u>may</u> be a storm overnight.   possible

The hero <u>might</u> save the villagers from the fearsome ogre.   possible

You <u>will</u> love the new track from this popular band.   certain

2 Rewrite each sentence using a different **modal verb** to change the meaning.

He <u>can</u> finish the race.   He might finish the race.

We <u>should</u> raise enough money.   We will raise enough money.

You <u>could</u> ask an adult to help you.   You must ask an adult to help you.

I <u>might</u> have cereal for breakfast.   I will have cereal for breakfast.

Sophie <u>might</u> swim 50 metres.   Sophie will swim 50 metres.

I <u>must</u> throw a six this time.   I may throw a six this time.

The pupils could use other modal verbs but those chosen should change the meaning of the sentence between certainty and possibility.

Sentence practice

Write <u>three</u> sentences about the future, using **modal verbs** to show different levels of possibility.

We might have flying cars. We could be living in space. We will all live longer.

25

These are just examples of sentences using modal verbs. You could discuss the choice of modal verbs with the pupils [e.g. why and how they have chosen to show certainty or possibility in each sentence].

Lesson 19 Verbs with suffixes

Focus converting nouns and adjectives into verbs using suffixes [–ify, –ise, –en, –ate]

Key terms verb, noun, adjective, suffix, root word

Focus text We classify materials as solids, liquids and gases. How would you categorise water?
Water is a liquid, but if we freeze it, water will solidify [harden] and form ice. If it is boiled, water will evaporate and form steam.

TEACH

Show the focus text and read it aloud. Discuss the changes in state described. Ask: What type of text is it taken from? [e.g. a science textbook; an explanation]

Discuss the meaning of the highlighted words [e.g. 'classify' – to put into a class; 'harden' – to become hard]. Point out that some of the words have the same or similar meanings [e.g. classify/categorise; solidify/harden]. Ask the pupils what type of word is highlighted [verbs – they describe actions/events].

Discuss how these verbs are formed. Identify the root word in each case [class, category, solid, hard, vapour]. Explain that these root words are nouns or adjectives. They are made into verbs by adding suffixes. Circle the suffixes added to the highlighted words [–ify, –ise, –en, –ate]. Remind the pupils that sometimes adding a suffix means the root word changes its spelling [e.g. category/categorise; vapour/evaporate].

Explain that the suffixes –ify, –ise, –en, –ate help to form useful verbs from nouns and adjectives [e.g. rather than saying 'it turns into a solid', we can say 'it solidifies']. Discuss other examples of verbs formed by using these suffixes [e.g. soft/soften; liquid/liquidise]. Invite the pupils to orally compose sentences using these verbs [e.g. Butter will soften if you put it somewhere warm. Liquidise the fruit.].

[Note: –ize is an acceptable alternative spelling of the suffix –ise: they are usually both shown in dictionaries.]

EXTEND Discuss more examples, using a dictionary to explore whether words are real or invented [e.g. certify; verify; truthify].

PRACTISE

Pupil book page 26

APPLY

- The pupils look for verbs with suffixes in other curriculum areas [e.g. science – 'magnify', 'electrify', 'pollinate'; design and technology – 'strengthen', 'widen', 'neaten'; history – 'civilise', 'colonise', 'fortify'].
- The pupils use dictionaries to find word families with nouns, adjectives and verbs formed from the same root word [e.g. terror – terrorist, terrible/terrific, terrify/terrorise].
- The pupils look for opportunities to use these verbs in speech and writing [e.g. Let's dramatise this scene. Let's finalise our list of ideas. Let's shorten this sentence.].

ASSESS

Dictation: Someone vandalised the leisure centre last night. Police are trying to identify two people seen earlier in the evening. Staff say they will tighten security while the police investigate.
Say: Underline the verbs formed with suffixes. Then see if you can write down a noun or an adjective that relates to each word.
Answer: e.g. vandal, identity, tight, investigation

Pupil book answers

Verbs with suffixes

Remember

Some **verbs** are formed from **nouns** or **adjectives** by adding **suffixes** (such as –ify, –ise, –en, –ate) to the **root words**. Sometimes the root word has to change its spelling.

solid → solid<u>ify</u>   hard → hard<u>en</u>

category → categor<u>ise</u>   vap<u>our</u> → evap<u>or</u>ate

Try it

1 Add a **suffix** to each noun or adjective to make a **verb**. Write the verb.

simple	<u>simplify</u>	straight	<u>straighten</u>
medic	<u>medicate</u>	pressure	<u>pressurise</u>
pure	<u>purify</u>	electric	<u>electrify</u>
captive	<u>captivate</u>	light	<u>lighten</u>
flat	<u>flatten</u>	active	<u>activate</u>
computer	<u>computerise</u>	equal	<u>equalise</u>

2 Complete each sentence with a **verb** formed from a noun or adjective in the box.

> **note   hard   critic   terror   strength   sympathy**

Exercise will <u>strengthen</u> your muscles.

I find it hard to <u>criticise</u> someone else's work.

The cement will <u>harden</u> as it dries out.

Some of the rides at theme parks <u>terrify</u> me.

Please <u>notify</u> the head teacher if your child is ill.

I can <u>sympathise</u> with your point of view.

Sentence practice

Write a sentence using **verbs** formed by adding **suffixes** to the words 'energy' and 'strength'.

<u>Exercise helps to energise you and strengthen your muscles.</u>

26

The verbs should be spelt correctly, including those that require a change to the spelling of the root word. If they are unsure, the pupils could use a dictionary to check their answers.

Accept words spelt –ize rather than –ise [e.g. pressurize; computerize].

The verbs should be spelt correctly, including those that require a change to the spelling of the root word. If the pupils use the verb 'terrorise' in the fourth sentence, point out that it does not fit the context of the sentence.

Accept words spelt –ize rather than –ise [criticize; sympathize].

This is just an example of a sentence that uses the verbs in a suitable context.

The verbs should be spelt correctly ['energise/energize' are both acceptable spellings].

Lesson 20 Verbs with prefixes

Focus understanding how prefixes [dis–, mis–, over–, re–, de–] change the meaning of verbs

Key terms prefix, verb, root word, word class

Focus text **Load** the machine. **Do not** overload it.
Connect the battery. **Always** disconnect it after use.
Let the machine fire up. **It may** misfire.
If so, reload the machine, reconnect the battery and retry.

TEACH

Display the focus text and read it aloud. Discuss what the instructions tell us to do to make the machine work. Establish the meaning of the highlighted words. Ask the pupils which word class the highlighted words belong to [verbs – they describe actions].

Discuss what the pupils notice about how these verbs are formed [e.g. by identifying root words and prefixes]. Circle the prefixes on the highlighted words [over–, dis–, mis–, re–]. Explain that prefixes like these are used to change the meaning of verbs. Discuss how each prefix changes the meaning of each verb in the focus text. For example, over– means to do something too much [load/overload]; dis– means to do the reverse or opposite [connect/disconnect]; mis– means to do something badly or wrongly [fire/misfire]; re– means to do again [reload, reconnect, retry].

Ask the pupils to suggest other examples of verbs with these prefixes, using a dictionary if necessary. Invite the pupils to say the word in a sentence to show that it is a verb [e.g. Discontinue using the machine.]. Explain that not all words with these prefixes are verbs. Ask: Is it an action? Does it have a tense? Discuss how the prefix changes the verb meaning, and note any variations [e.g. 'overlook' does not mean to look 'too much'].

Discuss other prefixes that can be used to change the meaning of verbs [e.g. un–; de–]. Again, invite the pupils to use them in sentences [e.g. Unlock the screen. Then debug the computer.].

EXTEND Discuss the use of hyphens with prefixes particularly to avoid ambiguity [e.g. recover/re-cover]. [Note: This topic is covered in detail in **Grammar 6**.]

PRACTISE

Pupil book page 27

APPLY

- The pupils collect examples and write definitions of verbs with these prefixes from different texts.
- Using dictionaries, the pupils find more examples of verbs with prefixes and use them in sentences.
- The pupils write dramatic headlines using verbs with the prefix over– [e.g. Ship overturns in storm; United overpowered in Cup; Plane overshoots runway].
- Discuss ideas for a story where something goes badly wrong. What might happen? [e.g. Does someone mishear, misbehave, miscount, miscalculate, misunderstand ...?]
- Ask the pupils to write their own instructions, using as many verbs with prefixes as they can.

ASSESS

Dictation: The goalkeeper overbalanced and the ball rebounded into the net. The referee allowed the goal, which pleased the manager.
Say: Underline two verbs with prefixes. Then add a prefix to two other verbs to change their meaning.
Answer: disallowed, displeased
Check: The verbs are spelt correctly.

Pupil book answers

Verbs with prefixes

Remember

When a **prefix** such as dis–, mis–, over–, re–, or de– is added to the beginning of a **verb**, it changes the meaning of the verb.

load
reload   (load it again)
overload (load it too much)

Try it

1   Add a **prefix** to each **verb** to change its meaning. Then write the meaning of the new verb.

___mis__behave	means	to behave badly
___over__flow	means	to flow over the top
___dis__continue	means	to not continue or to stop
___re__consider	means	to consider or to think again
___mis__calculate	means	to calculate wrongly
___re__pay	means	to pay back

2   Complete each sentence. Use the underlined **verb** again but change the **prefix**.

The magician <u>disappeared</u> but _then reappeared somewhere else._

Simply <u>inflate</u> the bouncy castle and _then deflate it after use._

Some shops <u>undercharged</u> their customers, _while others overcharged._

My teacher says that when you <u>miscount</u>, _you should always re-count the items._

You can easily <u>dehydrate</u> in hot weather, so _drink water to rehydrate._

Sentence practice

Write <u>three</u> sentences to give instructions for cooking something from the freezer. Use some **verbs** with **prefixes**.

First, defrost the item thoroughly. Do not undercook it or overcook it.

Do not refreeze it once cooked.

27

In the last two examples there is more than one acceptable answer. Check that the pupils give the appropriate meaning for their answer.

The pupils might end the sentences differently but they should use the required verbs. In the fourth sentence, 'discount' is not acceptable as it does not make sense in the context; 're-count' is usually written with a hyphen to avoid confusion with 'recount'. [Note: Hyphenation is covered in **Grammar 6**.]

The verbs should be spelt correctly. Adding prefixes requires no change to the spelling of the root word.

These are examples of possible instructions using verbs with prefixes. The verbs should be spelt correctly.

Check that the pupils have used commands to give instructions.

53

Revision 2 answers

Grammar 5

Focus: using –ly to turn adjectives into adverbs

The adverbs should be spelt correctly.

These are examples of correctly punctuated sentences showing an appropriate use of the adverbs. If an adverb is used at the front of the sentence, it should be followed by a comma.

This page focuses on aspects of vocabulary relating to the formation of words, which have been covered in earlier books.

The focus of each activity is given to help identify areas where the pupils might need further revision.

Revision 2

1 Write the **adverb** that can be formed from the **adjective**. Then write a sentence using the adverb you have made.

awkward	awkwardly	He landed awkwardly when he fell.
desperate	desperately	She fought desperately against the tide.
urgent	urgently	We need to speak to the head teacher urgently.
merry	merrily	Merrily, we strolled along.

Focus: regular plural-noun suffixes and irregular plurals

The plural words should be spelt correctly.

The last example is of a word that is the same in the plural as in the singular.

2 Write the **plural** form of each word.

question	questions	scientist	scientists
balcony	balconies	ox	oxen
address	addresses	calf	calves
volcano	volcanoes	salmon	salmon

Focus: forming nouns using suffixes

The nouns should be spelt correctly.

3 Complete each sentence with a **noun** formed from the verb in brackets.

Mum says she needs some rest and ___relaxation___ while on holiday.   (relax)

I have an important ___announcement___ to make.   (announce)

The school secretary says we need a paper ___shredder___ in the office.   (shred)

Focus: forming words using prefixes; word families

4 What does the **prefix** 'inter–' mean in the **word family** below? Tick <u>one</u>.

> interrupt   intervene   interfere   interface

beneath ☐   between ☑   above ☐   below ☐

5 What does the **root** 'locus' mean in the **word family** below? Tick <u>one</u>.

> local   location   locate   locomotive

long ☐   time ☐   place ☑   live ☐

28

Focus: word families; understanding how words are related in form and meaning

Remind the pupils to think about the shared meaning of the words.

This page focuses on identifying and using words from different word classes. The focus of each activity is given to help you identify terms that may need further revision.

Schofield & Sims **Grammar and Punctuation**   Grammar 5

6 Complete each sentence below with a **compound noun**.

I saw a ___buttercup___ in the garden.

We were playing in the ___playground___ .

The teachers were drinking tea in the ___staffroom___ .

7 Write a sentence using the word 'leak' as a **verb**.

I watched the water leak out of the tank.

Write a sentence using the word 'leak' as a **noun**.

There was a leak in the pipe.

8 Write a sentence using the word 'low' as an **adjective**.

The lorry could not get under the low bridge.

Write a sentence using the word 'low' as an **adverb**.

The eagle swooped low over the hillside.

9 Underline all the **adverbs** in the sentences below.

"It will <u>soon</u> be time to leave <u>here</u>," said the old man <u>sadly</u>.

Nadia told us <u>later</u> that she saw a fire engine <u>suddenly</u> pull up <u>outside</u>.

I have spent the money <u>already</u> and <u>therefore</u> we can't go to the cinema <u>now</u>.

10 Write a sentence for each **preposition** given below.

between   He slipped the letter between the pages of the book.

about   I read a book about a wizard.

behind   There was a man running behind the car.

through   She passed through a golden gate into the secret wood.

after   I started reading my new book after lunch.

on   He put a large slice of cake on his tray.

29

Focus: compound nouns

A compound noun should be formed from two root words. If the compound noun starts with a vowel, 'a' should change to 'an' [e.g. an earthworm].

Focus: verbs and nouns

This activity revises the idea that words can belong to different word classes, depending on the context.

Focus: adverbs and adjectives

Any correctly punctuated sentences are acceptable as long as the first sentence uses 'low' with a noun and the second uses it with a verb.

Focus: adverbs to express time/place/manner/cause

Check that the pupils identify all the adverbs, not just those ending with –ly. Remind them that the sentence should still make sense without the adverbs.

Focus: prepositions

These are just examples. Any correctly punctuated sentence using the given word as a preposition is acceptable. Compare the pupils' answers [e.g. some pupils might use 'between' to show time – 'between six and seven o'clock'].

Writing task 2: Analysis sheet

Pupil name: _____

Date: _____

Tick the circles to show amount of evidence found in writing: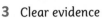
1 No evidence
2 Some evidence
3 Clear evidence

Assessing punctuation

The writing sample demonstrates:	Evidence		
sentence boundaries demarcated with capital letters and appropriate end punctuation.	①	②	③
capital letters used for 'I' and proper nouns.	①	②	③
commas used to separate items in a list [e.g. names; short phrases], as well as after fronted adverbials and before question tags.	①	②	③
apostrophes used correctly in contractions and for possession [e.g. the town's one-way system].	①	②	③
direct speech puncuated correctly, including when spoken words are split.	①	②	③
the use of punctuation to indicate parenthesis [commas, brackets or dashes].	①	②	③

Assessing grammar and sentence structure

The writing sample demonstrates:	Evidence		
grammatically correct sentences that show variation and use Standard English [e.g. verbs; agreement; pronouns].	①	②	③
expanded noun phrases to convey information concisely [e.g. a stunning shot from outside the penalty area].	①	②	③
adverbials to add detail about where, when, why or how [e.g. last night during the rush hour] and to vary sentence openings.	①	②	③
subordinate clauses, using a wide range of conjunctions to link clauses or ideas.	①	②	③
pronouns to avoid repetition and aid cohesion, with no ambiguity.	①	②	③
varied use of verb forms to express time, including progressive and perfect forms [e.g. The police had taken ...].	①	②	③
relative clauses, to add information or ideas [e.g. The driver of the lorry, who was not badly injured, ...].	①	②	③
modal verbs to express possibility or future events [e.g. There might be an investigation.].	①	②	③

Key target: _____

Writing task 2: Pupil checklist

Name: _____   Date: _____

Reread what you have written to check that it makes sense. Tick the circle if you have correctly used the punctuation or grammar feature in your writing.

Punctuation

◯ I have used capital letters at the beginning of sentences, and full stops, question marks or exclamation marks at the end of sentences.

◯ I have used capital letters for 'I' and proper nouns.

◯ I have used commas to separate items in a list.

◯ I have used apostrophes in contractions and for possession.

◯ I have used inverted commas and other punctuation in direct speech.

◯ I have used commas after fronted adverbials and before question tags.

◯ I have used punctuation to indicate parenthesis (commas, brackets or dashes).

Grammar and sentences

◯ I have used grammatically correct sentences and Standard English.

◯ I have used different types of sentence and different sentence openings.

◯ I have used expanded noun phrases to describe and give details.

◯ I have used adverbials to add detail about where, when, how and why.

◯ I have used sentences with subordinate clauses and a range of conjunctions.

◯ I have used pronouns and it is clear who or what they refer to.

◯ I have used different verb forms to express past time, with some progressive and perfect forms.

◯ I have used relative clauses to add detail about nouns.

◯ I have used modal verbs to suggest possibilities or future events.

Teacher feedback

My key target: _____

_____

*From: **Grammar 5 Teacher's Guide** © Schofield & Sims Ltd, 2017. This page may be photocopied after purchase.*

Lesson 21 Commas within sentences

Focus   using commas to separate elements of a sentence

Key terms   comma, phrase, clause, main clause, subordinate clause, question tag, adverbial, parenthesis, direct speech

Focus text   The stairs creaked, I sat up with a start. I had locked the door, hadn't I?
"Dad, is that you?" I called into the darkness.
There was no answer. I thought perhaps I was dreaming.
Then, out of the silence, I heard another creak. Someone, or something, was out there. Clutching the duvet, I huddled in bed.

TEACH

Show the focus text and read it aloud. Discuss the situation, the character's feelings, what sort of story it might be [e.g. adventure story; ghost story] and what might happen next. Invite the pupils to comment on grammar that helps make it effective [e.g. different sentence types – questions, short sentences, fronted adverbials; words to create uncertainty – 'someone', 'something', 'perhaps'].

Ask the pupils to identify all the commas in the focus text. Circle them.

Explain that commas have a number of uses but they are always used *within* sentences. They cannot be used between two separate sentences or main clauses. Ask the pupils to spot the incorrect use of a comma in the focus text [in the first sentence]. Explain that both 'The stairs creaked' and 'I sat up with a start' are main clauses, so they should be punctuated as two separate sentences. Add the full stop after 'creaked'.

Explain that commas are used to show breaks between parts of a sentence [e.g. separate words, phrases or clauses]. Discuss why each comma is needed in the focus text [to separate a question tag or the name of the person being addressed; after a fronted adverbial; to show parenthesis].

Invite the pupils to suggest other uses of commas and orally compose some sentences for the focus text to illustrate these [e.g. lists – 'I heard one step, two steps, three steps …'; direct speech – "Go away," I said.].

EXTEND   Discuss punctuation marks that can be used between two main clauses [e.g. semicolon]. [Note: Semicolons are covered in **Grammar 6**.]

PRACTISE

Pupil book page 32

APPLY

- The pupils write a scene between characters, demonstrating different uses of commas [e.g. for direct speech; question tags; after names, adding actions to speech – 'hissed Ben, gripping my arm'].
- The pupils write stories using fronted adverbials with commas to slow the pace and build tension, and commas to indicate parenthesis.
- Discuss possible uses of commas with the pupils before they write non-fiction texts [e.g. in lists; for parenthesis; after fronted adverbials]. Encourage them to use an example of each in their writing.

ASSESS

Dictation: The tiger, one of the biggest and most powerful of the big cats, lives in the forests of Asia. Unlike lions, tigers live alone. Generally, they sleep by day and hunt by night. Their main foods are antelope, buffalo, deer and wild pigs.
Check: The sentence boundaries are correct, as well as the commas.

Pupil book answers

Grammar 5

Schofield & Sims **Grammar and Punctuation**

Commas within sentences

Remember

Commas have a number of uses but they are always used <u>within</u> a sentence. They are used to show breaks between different parts of a sentence (for example, in **lists**, with **question tags**, in **direct speech**, in **parentheses** and after **fronted adverbials**). They can separate words, phrases or clauses.

"Dad, is that you?" I called into the darkness.
Then, out of the silence, I heard another creak. Someone, or something, was out there. Clutching the duvet, I huddled in bed.

You could ask the pupils to explain why the comma was needed in a particular place. This would help to check their understanding and prepare for the second activity.

Try it

1 Insert **commas** in the correct place(s) in each sentence.

"Come here," she said, "and tell me again."

The sense of touch means I can feel if things are hot, cold, soft, hard, smooth or rough.

Carbohydrates, such as starch and sugar, give us energy.

Without warning, the huge bird swooped down and grabbed him.

Wherever she went that day, the cat seemed to follow her.

Have you been snowboarding before, Emma?

2 Explain why a **comma** is used in each sentence.

I've told you this story before, haven't I?

It separates the question tag from the main sentence.

When the sun is high in the sky, there is nothing better than a picnic by the river.

It separates the fronted subordinate clause from the main clause.

Poor Chris, who is allergic to cats, began to sneeze.

It separates the extra information (or parenthesis) added into the sentence.

The pupils do not need to use terms such as 'parenthesis' but they should explain the use of the comma(s) in that particular sentence. General answers such as 'to separate the parts of the sentence' or 'to separate the words off' are not adequate. Ask the pupils *why* they need separating.

Sentence practice

Write <u>two</u> sentences about someone going into a mysterious house. Use one or more **commas** in each sentence.

After a quick glance over her shoulder, she put the key in the lock and opened the door. Quickly, she slipped inside.

32

This is just an example of two sentences using commas. The pupils can develop the subject matter in any way they choose and could demonstrate other uses of commas [e.g. in direct speech; with question tags].

Check sentence punctuation as well as the use of commas, making sure that commas are not used to separate sentences or main clauses, which can continue to be a problem.

Lesson 22 Commas to avoid ambiguity

Focus using commas to clarify meaning and avoid ambiguity

Key terms comma, ambiguity

Focus text Keep tackling Joe.   Keep tackling, Joe.
Stop children crossing.   Stop, children crossing.
The things I like best are cooking my dog and music.

TEACH

Show the first two sentences of the focus text. Ask the pupils to spot the difference between them [the comma in the second sentence]. Read the sentences aloud using appropriate intonation for each one. Ask the pupils to explain how the use of the comma changes the meaning of the sentences [e.g. without the comma, it sounds like we are being told to keep tackling someone called Joe; with the comma, it sounds like Joe is being told to keep tackling].

Explain that as well as separating parts of a sentence, commas are also important because they help to make the meaning of a sentence clear. They help to avoid ambiguity or uncertainty about the intended meanings, as in the focus text.

Show the next two sentences. Again, they are the same apart from a comma. Read the sentences aloud, with a pause after the comma in the second sentence. Ask the pupils to explain the different meanings of the sentences [e.g. without the comma, we are told to stop *children* from crossing; with the comma, *we* are told to stop because children are crossing]. Discuss which is the intended meaning [the second one, so the comma is needed to make this meaning clear].

Show the last sentence of the focus text. Read it aloud and discuss the humour created by the lack of a comma [it sounds as if the writer likes cooking their dog]. Ask the pupils where the comma should be inserted in order to make the meaning clear and avoid ambiguity [after 'cooking'].

Invite the pupils to orally compose another example to show how a comma can change the meaning of a sentence based on those shown [e.g. "Are you cooking, Dad?"/"Are you cooking Dad?"].

EXTEND Discuss how using commas with relative clauses can change the meaning [e.g. The children, who had crossed the road, were safe./The children who had crossed the road were safe.]. [Note: This is covered in **Grammar 6**.]

PRACTISE

Pupil book page 33

APPLY

- Remind the pupils to orally rehearse sentences before writing them, so that they can hear where commas are needed. They should then reread sentences once written, to check that the commas are in the right place.
- Make it a proofreading target to check for ambiguity and add commas to clarify meaning.

ASSESS

Dictation: Have you met my sister, James? She likes sleeping, cats and reading.
Say: Explain how missing out the commas in these sentences would change the meaning.
Answer: e.g. Without the commas it would mean a sister called James who likes sleeping cats.

Pupil book answers

Commas to avoid ambiguity

Remember

Commas are important – sometimes they can change the meaning of a sentence.

Keep tackling Joe.   Keep tackling, Joe.

Commas make the meaning of a sentence clear and prevent any ambiguity or misunderstanding. Think what this sentence would mean without the comma!

The things I like best are cooking, my dog and music.

Try it

1. Explain how the **commas** change the meaning in each pair of sentences.

   No tickets are available.   No, tickets are available.

   With the comma, there are tickets available to buy.

   Without the comma, there are no tickets available to buy.

   Lola was a pretty smart girl.   Lola was a pretty, smart girl.

   With the comma, Lola is pretty and smart. Without the comma, she is
   'pretty smart', or quite clever.

   > The pupils should explain the meaning in *both* sentences in their answers – i.e. referring to the sentence both with and without the comma.

2. Rewrite each sentence using a **comma** to clarify the meaning.

   After he ate the lion was full.   After he ate, the lion was full.

   I'm starving. Let's eat Mum.   I'm starving. Let's eat, Mum.

   Above a seagull squawked loudly.   Above, a seagull squawked loudly.

   To Callum James seemed bold.   To Callum, James seemed bold.

   Are we going to paint Miss Jones?   Are we going to paint, Miss Jones?

   I like collecting sports and   I like collecting, sports and watching films.

   watching films.

   > You could ask the pupils to explain the ambiguity in the original sentence and why the comma is needed.

Sentence practice

Write <u>two</u> versions of a sentence to show how a **comma** can change the meaning.

I ate chocolate cake and sandwiches.

I ate chocolate, cake and sandwiches.

33

> This is just one paired example. If necessary, encourage the pupils to use one of the sentences on the page as a model. Compare the pupils' answers. Ask them to explain how the comma changes the meaning in their own or another sentence.

Lesson 23 Linking paragraphs using adverbials

> Focus linking ideas across paragraphs using linking adverbials to show time, place, number
>
> Key terms paragraph, adverbial, **cohesion**
>
> Focus text We would like to offer some suggestions for improving the school playground.
> Firstly, we would like you to consider providing new equipment.
> Secondly, we could set up a quiet area in the school grounds.
> Finally, ...
> These suggestions would really improve the playground.

TEACH

Show the focus text. Explain that this is an outline plan for a piece of non-fiction writing. Read the first sentence. Discuss the purpose and intended audience [e.g. to persuade the head teacher to improve the playground].

Read the opening sentences of paragraphs 1 and 2. Discuss the main idea in each. Invite the pupils to offer a final suggestion to complete the plan [Finally, ...].

Remind the pupils that we organise our writing into a series of paragraphs that develop our ideas in a logical order. Sometimes this order is determined by time or place [e.g. in a story or account] or by subject [e.g. different aspects of a subject in a factual text]. In the focus text, each paragraph presents one point or idea relating to the main theme [improving the playground].

Explain that we use linking adverbials like those highlighted to show the reader how the paragraphs fit or link together. This helps to connect ideas together and give the text cohesion. In a story or account, we use adverbials of time or place [e.g. Later, ...; Nearby, ...] but in the focus text the adverbials number and order the points. Discuss possible alternatives [e.g. First of all, ...; In addition, ...; Furthermore, ...].

Discuss how the last sentence connects to the rest of the text and helps to give the text cohesion [e.g. it refers back to the main theme; it uses 'these suggestions' to refer back to the points made].

EXTEND Discuss how the repetition of words and phrases, and the use of alternative nouns, can also help to link ideas and give the text cohesion [e.g. school playground/school grounds].

PRACTISE

Pupil book page 34

APPLY

- When writing stories, the pupils use adverbials of time or place to link ideas across paragraphs.
- When writing descriptions of real or imaginary places, the pupils use adverbials of place to guide the reader round the location [e.g. Nearby ...; Beside ...; On the other side ...].
- The pupils present a point of view or a number of suggestions, orally or in writing, using adverbials.
- Discuss with the pupils adverbials used in different types of text [e.g. procedures; explanations].

ASSESS

Dictation: Should parents restrict the time children spend using electronic devices?
Say: Plan a piece of writing based on this theme. Write the first sentence for each paragraph, developing the theme and using adverbials to link ideas across the paragraphs.

Pupil book answers

Linking paragraphs using adverbials

Remember

You can use **paragraphs** to develop your ideas in a piece of writing. Linking **adverbials** can be used at the start of paragraphs to make it clear how your ideas fit together. This helps to give the text cohesion.

We would like to offer some suggestions to improve the school playground. Firstly, we would like you to consider providing new equipment. Secondly, we could set up a quiet area.

Try it

1. Underline the **adverbials** that show how each pair of ideas links together.

   <u>Outside the cabin</u>, you can enjoy the woodland setting.
   <u>Inside</u>, you will find a welcoming fire and everything you need.

   <u>To begin with</u>, we will grow vegetables in pots and containers.
   <u>After that</u>, we hope to have a small vegetable patch in the school grounds.

   <u>First of all</u>, make sure that you have all the necessary safety equipment.
   <u>Secondly</u>, check the weather forecast before you set out.

   <u>On the one hand</u>, firework displays can be thrilling to watch.
   <u>On the other hand</u>, many people are injured by fireworks every year.

2. Plan a piece of non-fiction writing with the title: 'Water is more precious than gold'. Write the <u>first</u> sentence for each **paragraph**, using **adverbials** to link your ideas.

   Introduction: Water is definitely more precious than gold.

   Firstly, we cannot live without water.

   Secondly, water is essential for growing food.

   Thirdly, clean water is vital for hygiene and to stop diseases.

   Furthermore, industry and manufacturing need water.

   In conclusion, I think these reasons show that water is more precious than gold.

Sentence practice

Make a plan for a piece of non-fiction writing, persuading people to support your favourite charity. Write the <u>first</u> sentence for each **paragraph**. Write your plan on a separate piece of paper.

34

You may wish to discuss what type of text these sentences might come from and how the rest of the text might develop [e.g. giving different views on fireworks].

These are just examples of arguments the pupils might make. Each sentence should clearly state the point to be made in the paragraph. Check that the pupils have used adverbials to link ideas across the paragraphs [e.g. Firstly, ...; Secondly, ...]. They could use various linking adverbials [e.g. Furthermore, ...; Moreover, ...].

Look also for a conclusion that links back to the earlier points [e.g. For these reasons, ...].

Each sentence should clearly state the point to be made in the paragraph. Adverbials should be used to link ideas across the paragraphs [e.g. Firstly, ...; Secondly, ...; In addition, ...; Furthermore, ...].

Look for a concluding sentence that links back to the main idea of supporting the charity [e.g. For these reasons, ...].

Lesson 24 Linking ideas within paragraphs

Focus using devices to build cohesion within a paragraph – adverbials, pronouns and conjunctions

Key terms paragraph, cohesion, adverbial, pronoun, conjunction

Focus text One suggestion is that we start a gardening club. We could grow our own vegetables and then sell them or eat them ourselves. <u>For example</u>, we could grow tomatoes in pots or potatoes in sacks. This would not be too expensive. It would, <u>however</u>, require the help of an adult. <u>Therefore</u>, we were going to ask parents if they would like to help.

TEACH

Show the focus text. Explain that this is a paragraph from a text discussing ideas for after-school clubs. Remind the pupils that a paragraph should have a clear focus, which is clearly introduced in the first sentence. Ask the pupils to identify the focus of this paragraph [a possible gardening club].

Read the paragraph and discuss how the idea is developed [e.g. explaining the idea; giving examples; justifying; recognising potential problems and giving suggestions for how to solve them].

Explain that within a paragraph, ideas should be developed in a logical order. It is important to show the reader how the ideas link together to give the paragraph cohesion. For example, we can use adverbials to link sentences. Ask the pupils to identify linking adverbials used in the focus text and discuss what they show [e.g. 'for example' signals an illustration of the preceding point; 'therefore' shows reasons or results; 'however' shows opposition or a counter-argument].

Explain that the linking adverbial does not always have to go at the start of a sentence. It can be included within a sentence, using commas [e.g. It would, <u>however</u>, require the help of an adult.].

Discuss other words that help to build cohesion within the paragraph in the focus text [e.g. the use of conjunctions to link ideas within sentences – 'and', 'or', 'if'; the use of pronouns to refer back to previous ideas – 'and sell <u>them</u>', '<u>This</u> would not be …', '<u>It</u> would, however, …'].

EXTEND Discuss alternatives to the adverbials used in the focus text [e.g. however – on the other hand; therefore – consequently/as a result/for that reason; for example – for instance].

PRACTISE

Pupil book page 35

APPLY

- When they are writing factual texts, the pupils structure paragraphs by beginning with a topic sentence and then developing the idea with supportive detail, explanation and example. They use linking adverbials [e.g. for example; therefore; however] and pronouns [e.g. <u>This</u> means …].
- As they write, encourage the pupils to keep rereading to check cohesion within a paragraph.
- When they are reviewing their own writing, encourage the pupils to make changes to improve the cohesion within a paragraph [e.g. adding linking adverbials to sentences; using conjunctions to link ideas within a sentence; using pronouns to link ideas within and across sentences].

ASSESS

Dictation: At the kennels, they look after many dogs that have been rescued from neglect.
Say: This is the first sentence from a paragraph. Write the rest of the paragraph using adverbials, conjunctions and pronouns to build cohesion.

Pupil book answers

Linking ideas within paragraphs

Remember

Within a **paragraph**, you need to show how the ideas link together, to make it clear and give it cohesion. You can use **adverbials** to show the links between sentences, and **pronouns** to refer back to previous ideas.

We could grow our own vegetables and then sell them. For example, we could grow tomatoes in pots or potatoes in sacks. This would not be too expensive.

Try it

1. Underline the **adverbials** and circle the **pronouns** that help to link the ideas between each pair of sentences.

   The T-shirt is made of a special fabric that helps to keep you cool. In addition, (this) is very hard-wearing.

   We have complained many times about the overflowing rubbish bins. (They) are still outside our school, however.

   Anna Sewell's only book, Black Beauty, was published in 1878. Soon after that, (she) died, without knowing how successful (it) would be.

   We found that children had different opinions about e-readers. (Some,) for example, liked the convenience of an e-reader, while (others) preferred an old-fashioned book.

2. Write a sentence to follow the given sentence. Use **adverbials** and/or **pronouns** to link the sentences together.

   The park has facilities suitable for children of all ages. _For example, there is a spacious playground for younger children._

   In some countries, large areas of rainforest have been destroyed. _As a result, some animals that live there have become endangered species._

   Some children may argue that they need their mobile phone in class. _However, teachers would say that they are a distraction._

Sentence practice

Write a **paragraph** about an idea for an after-school club at your school. Use **adverbials** and **pronouns** to link your ideas together. Write the paragraph on a separate piece of paper.

35

Check that the pupils recognise linking adverbials that are not at the beginning of sentences [e.g. Some, for example, ...].

You could discuss what the pronouns refer back to [e.g. 'This' = the fabric; 'They' = the bins]. Remind the pupils how important it is to make clear what the pronouns refer to.

These are just examples of sentences that could follow the given sentences. The pupils may have developed the ideas in a different way. Look for the use of a linking adverbial to show how the idea is being developed, and/or a pronoun to refer back to the given sentence [e.g. live 'there'; 'they' are a distraction].

Look for a cohesive paragraph with an opening sentence to introduce the idea and then a series of linked sentences to develop it. Look for the use of adverbials to link sentences and conjunctions within sentences. Look also for pronouns referring back to previous nouns or ideas.

Lesson 25 Standard English: adverbs

Focus using Standard English forms of adverbs [e.g. –ly adverbs]

Key terms adverb, adjective, verb, noun, Standard English, non-Standard English

Focus text What did you think of the athletes' performances today?
Well, I thought Zain ran quick in his race.
Yeah, Jess done good to reach the final.
Ben were in a real difficult heat.

TEACH

Show the focus text and read it aloud. Discuss the situation and who is speaking [e.g. pundits/ commentators on a sports programme]. Establish that it is spoken language rather than written.

Remind the pupils that sometimes people use non-Standard English in speech. Ask them to identify examples of non-Standard English words in the focus text [e.g. 'Yeah'; verbs 'done', 'were']. Ask the pupils to change these words to the Standard English forms [Yes, did, was]. Remind them that we nearly always write in Standard English.

If the pupils have not already spotted them, underline the examples of adjectives used as adverbs in the focus text [ran quick, did good, real difficult]. Ask the pupils to explain why these phrases do not sound right. Explain that the underlined words are adjectives but they are being used as adverbs in these sentences [e.g. to say *how* the athletes performed, or to strengthen an adjective].

Explain that adjectives can only be used to modify nouns; they cannot be used with verbs or other adjectives. Confusion often occurs because many 'how' adverbs are formed by adding –ly to an adjective [e.g. quick/quickly; real/really]. In Standard English, it is important to use the adverb form of the word with verbs or other adjectives [e.g. 'quickly' rather than 'quick'].

Discuss the adverb needed in each sentence of the focus text [quickly, well, really]. Remind the pupils that 'good' is an adjective we use with a noun [e.g. Jess had a good race] but 'well' is the adverb form, rather than 'goodly' [e.g. she did well].

EXTEND Discuss examples where adjectives and adverbs are the same [e.g. she ran hard/it was a hard race; she jumped high/it was a high jump].

PRACTISE

Pupil book page 36

APPLY

- The pupils write a sporting commentary demonstrating the use of non-Standard English, including adjectives used as adverbs. They then rewrite it using Standard English.
- When writing stories, the pupils use a range of adverbs formed from adjectives to describe actions and convey character [e.g. bowed graciously/elegantly; spoke impatiently/spitefully].
- Remind the pupils to use Standard adverb forms in other areas of the curriculum [e.g. design and technology – 'we tied it tightly'].
- Encourage the pupils to orally rehearse sentences using Standard English before writing them down.

ASSESS

Dictation: You have done good this afternoon. Now, let's clear up real quick so we can finish that story before home time.
Say: Underline any examples of non-Standard English. Then rewrite the sentences using Standard English.
Answer: … done well …; clear up really quickly …

Pupil book answers

Standard English: adverbs

Remember

Sometimes people use **adjectives** instead of **adverbs** when they speak. This is not **Standard English**. In writing, you should use adverbs to describe verbs or other adjectives.

Zain <u>ran quick</u> in his race. ✗   Zain <u>ran quickly</u> in his race. ✓

Jess <u>did good</u> to reach the final. ✗   Jess <u>did well</u> to reach the final. ✓

Ben was in a <u>real difficult</u> heat. ✗   Ben was in a <u>really difficult</u> heat. ✓

Try it

1 Choose the word from the brackets that completes each sentence using **Standard English**.

　　_____Luckily_____ , she reached the cliff edge just in time.   (lucky luckily)

　　We need to think ___seriously___ about this problem.   (seriously serious)

　　He dressed ___smartly___ for the occasion.   (smart smartly)

　　The parrot squawked ___loudly___ all morning.   (loud loudly)

　　They played ___well___ in the first half.   (well good)

　　The deafening roar lessened ___gradually___ .   (gradually gradual)

> 'Luckily' should have a capital letter.

2 Rewrite each sentence using the **Standard English** form of all words.

She done it beautiful.	She did it beautifully.
The wind blowed real gentle.	The wind blew really gently.
The concert were well good.	The concert was very good.
I tries to eat healthy.	I try to eat healthily.
It were a fair big mistake.	It was a fairly big mistake.
I should have writ the note proper.	I should have written the note properly.

> The adverbs ending with –ly should be spelt correctly. Check that the pupils have also used Standard English verb forms. Use this opportunity to discuss any local spoken verb forms that your pupils use in their writing.

Sentence practice

Write a sentence using the **adjective** 'terrible', and a sentence using the **adverb** formed from it.

adjective　___I had a terrible pain.___

adverb　___We played terribly in the second half.___

> These are just examples of sentences using the adjective 'terrible' and the adverb 'terribly'. Check that 'terrible' is used with a noun, and 'terribly' with a verb [e.g. played terribly] or adjective [e.g. terribly loud].
>
> The adverb 'terribly' should be spelt correctly.

Lesson 26 **Sentence adverbs**

Focus using adverbs to comment on a whole sentence

Key terms adverb, comma

Focus text **Dad said we had approximately half an hour to thoroughly clean the kitchen before Mum arrived home.
Really, he should know better.
Fortunately, Mum was delayed by bad traffic. Surprisingly, even then she didn't seem to notice the mess hidden in the cupboards.**

TEACH

Show the focus text and read it aloud. Discuss the situation [e.g. Why was it fortunate that Mum was delayed?]. Discuss what type of text these sentences might be taken from [e.g. a first-person story; a diary]. Identify features in the text that show it is a personal account [e.g. the use of 'we'; the writer's comments on events – 'Really, he should know better.'].

Discuss what type of word is highlighted [adverbs]. Remind the pupils that we often use adverbs to show where, when or how [e.g. <u>thoroughly</u> clean the kitchen] or to modify other words [e.g. <u>approximately</u> half an hour]. However, adverbs can also be used to comment on a whole sentence. Ask the pupils to find examples of this in the focus text [the sentences starting with 'Really', 'Fortunately', 'Surprisingly'].

Explain that in these sentences the adverbs comment on the whole sentence. They show the attitude or view of the writer on what the sentence tells us. For example, in the sentence '<u>Fortunately</u>, Mum was delayed by bad traffic.', 'Fortunately' gives the writer's personal comment on Mum's delay. Mum probably did not think it was fortunate, but the writer does.

Explain that these adverbs are often placed at the start of the sentence, followed by a comma. Invite the pupils to orally construct some more sentences starting with these or similar adverbs [e.g. Unfortunately, Dad …]. Discuss moving the adverbs to different positions in the sentence and the implications of this for punctuation [e.g. Mum was delayed, fortunately, …/Mum, fortunately, was delayed …].

EXTEND Discuss the need to use commas to avoid ambiguity when using adverbs at the end of sentences [e.g. Mum's arrival made the dog bark, strangely./… made the dog bark strangely.].

PRACTISE

Pupil book page 37

APPLY

- The pupils write diary entries using sentence adverbs to comment or give a personal view of events.
- When writing in role, the pupils use sentence adverbs to show the attitude of the writer to events.
- In stories, the pupils use sentence adverbs to build suspense, to suggest something to come [e.g. Surprisingly, …; Astonishingly, …] or to introduce a possible complication [e.g. Unfortunately, …].
- The pupils use sentence adverbs to show a viewpoint when writing an argument [e.g. Sadly, …].
- Discuss the appropriate use of sentence adverbs to show the author's viewpoint in other non-fiction texts [e.g. in biographies to comment on a person's achievements – 'Remarkably, …'].

ASSESS

Dictation: <u>Unfortunately</u>, I am in Miss Smith's class next year. What a disaster! <u>Seriously</u>, she is the strictest teacher in the school. <u>Thankfully</u>, Leo is in the same class so we can suffer together.
Say: Underline any sentence adverbs.
Check: There are commas after the fronted adverbials and the sentence punctuation is correct.

Pupil book answers

Sentence adverbs

Remember

Adverbs are used to add detail about how, where, when or how often events happen. However, you can also use adverbs to add a comment on a whole sentence. These adverbs are often fronted, or placed at the start of the sentence.

Fortunately, Mum was delayed by bad traffic.
Surprisingly, she didn't notice the mess.

Try it

1 Complete each sentence using a suitable **adverb** from the box. Punctuate it correctly.

> amazingly   interestingly   sadly   surprisingly   unfortunately

___Amazingly,___ the next day the cupboard was full again.

___Unfortunately,___ a number of paintings have been damaged in the flood.

___Interestingly,___ people could not tell the difference between the two ice creams.

___Sadly,___ he was too ill to go to Sunil's party.

___Surprisingly,___ it sometimes snows even in spring.

2 Complete each sentence, using the given **adverb** to comment or add meaning.

Luckily, he had time to get out before the fire spread.

Strangely, he didn't remember anything about the events.

Obviously, exercise is good for you.

Incredibly, they escaped from the accident unhurt.

Curiously, no-one seems to have heard anything.

Personally, I think this is a really bad decision.

Sentence practice

Write two sentences, one to introduce a problem and one about solving the problem. Use the **adverbs** 'unfortunately' and 'fortunately'.

Unfortunately, all the apples fell on to the floor. Fortunately, there were lots of people to help pick them up.

37

Other adverbs would work with many of the sentences [e.g. sadly/ unfortunately; interestingly/ surprisingly]. You could compare choices, discussing how the adverb comments on the sentence [e.g. that the writer thinks it was amazing/unfortunate/ interesting].

The adverbs should begin with a capital letter and be followed by a comma, since they are at the start of a sentence.

These are just examples of sentences using the given sentence adverbs.

Compare the pupils' sentences and discuss how each adverb makes a comment or adds meaning.

These are just examples of possible sentences using the adverbs to comment in a suitable context.

The sentences should be punctuated correctly, each including a comma to separate the adverb from the rest of the sentence. If the pupils have used the adverb elsewhere, the sentence should still be punctuated correctly [e.g. There were lots of people, fortunately, to help pick them up.].

Lesson 27 **Word classes**

> Focus identifying conjunctions/prepositions, pronouns/determiners by how they are used
>
> Key terms word class, conjunction, preposition, phrase, clause, pronoun, determiner
>
> Focus text I left <u>before</u> the end of the match.   Indicate <u>before</u> you turn left.
> I see her every day, standing outside her flat.
> She told me to post this in that box.

TEACH

Show the first two sentences and read them aloud. Ask the pupils which words appear in both sentences [left, before]. Discuss what they notice about how these words are used in the sentences ['left' is a verb in the first sentence and an adverb in the second; 'before' is a preposition in the first sentence and a conjunction in the second].

Remind the pupils that we group words into word classes according to how they are used in sentences. The word classes are noun, verb, adjective, adverb, preposition, determiner, pronoun and conjunction. However, a word can belong in more than one class depending on how it is used in a sentence.

Explain that 'before', in particular, is a word with different uses. Discuss how it is used in the two sentences above. In the first sentence, 'before' is used at the start of a *phrase* [before <u>the end of the match</u>], so it is a preposition. In the second sentence, it is used to start a subordinate *clause* [before <u>you turn left</u>], so it is a conjunction. We need to look at what comes *after* the word to see if it is a conjunction or a preposition. Discuss other examples of sentences using 'before' as a conjunction and as a preposition.

Show the other sentences in the focus text. Discuss the highlighted words. Explain that some words [e.g. his/her; this/that] can be either determiners or pronouns, depending on how they are used in the sentence. If the word is used before a noun, it is a determiner [<u>her</u> flat, <u>that</u> box]; if it *replaces* a noun, so there is no noun after it, it is a pronoun [I see <u>her</u>, post <u>this</u>].

The sentences in the focus text also contain other examples of words that could be used in different ways in other sentences. Ask the pupils to give examples [e.g. 'match' and 'box' could be verbs rather than nouns; 'post' could be a noun rather than a verb; 'flat' could be an adjective rather than a noun].

EXTEND Discuss the fact that 'before' and 'flat' could also be adverbs [e.g. I have been here before. The puppy was lying flat on its back.].

PRACTISE

Pupil book page 38

APPLY

- Use the terms 'preposition' and 'conjunction', or 'determiner' and 'pronoun', when discussing writing and encourage the pupils to use them too.
- Explore with the pupils any entries in dictionaries that show when words can belong to different word classes. The pupils then collect examples of these 'multi-tasking words'.
- In other curriculum areas, the pupils look for words that can be used in different ways [e.g. cycle; cutting; spring].

ASSESS

Dictation: <u>After</u> Greta left <u>her</u> house, Emily followed <u>her</u> <u>down</u> the road.
Say: Underline the words 'after', 'her', 'her' [again] and 'down'. Then label them to show the word class they belong to.
Answer: 'after' = conjunction; 'her [house]' = determiner; '[followed] her' = pronoun; 'down' = preposition

Pupil book answers

Word classes

Remember

Some words belong to more than one **word class**, depending on how they are used in the sentence. For example, 'before' can be either a **conjunction** (before a clause) or a **preposition** (before a phrase).

I left before it finished. (conjunction)   I left before the end. (preposition)

Similarly, 'her' can be either a **pronoun** or a **determiner**.

I see her every day. (pronoun)   I see her friend every day. (determiner)

Try it

1   Read each sentence. Is the underlined word a **conjunction** or a **preposition**?

We went for a walk <u>since</u> the sun was shining.   conjunction

I have not seen Jade <u>since</u> nine o'clock this morning.   preposition

Let's keep going <u>until</u> the car runs out of petrol.   conjunction

You will stay here <u>until</u> the end of time.   preposition

Read each sentence. Is the underlined word a **determiner** or a **pronoun**?

Mum gave me these grapes but I already had <u>some</u> at lunchtime.   pronoun

I saw <u>some</u> lovely clothes in the shops on Saturday.   determiner

Put <u>those</u> red apples in the bowl over there.   determiner

Would you like to try <u>those</u> on?   pronoun

2   Write a sentence using 'after' as a **conjunction**. Then use it as a **preposition**.

conjunction   We can play football after we finish doing our homework.

preposition   I asked Mum to collect me after football practice.

Write a sentence using 'this' as a **determiner**. Then use it as a **pronoun**.

determiner   I found this dog in the playground.

pronoun   Can you put this in the bin for me?

Sentence practice

Write a sentence using 'before' as a **conjunction** and 'these' as a **pronoun**.

Before I saw those new trainers, I thought these were the best.

38

Remind the pupils to check what comes after the word. A conjunction is followed by a clause [with a verb]; a preposition by a phrase [with no verb].

The pupils should check whether there is a noun [or noun phrase] after the word. If so, then the word is being used as a determiner. If not, it is being used as a pronoun.

These are just examples of sentences showing the different uses of the words. Check that the words are used correctly each time.

This is an example of a sentence that uses 'before' to begin a subordinate clause, and 'these' as a pronoun. Check that 'before' comes at the start of a clause, not a phrase, and that 'these' is used as a pronoun replacing a noun ['trainers' in this example] rather than as a determiner [e.g. these trainers].

Lesson 28 **Possessives**

Focus using possessive pronouns and apostrophes to show possession

Key terms noun, possessive pronoun, **possessive noun**, apostrophe, determiner

Focus text Should we be concerned about the planet's future? As the world's population increases and the Earth's natural resources decrease, what will happen? Should we listen to environmentalists' concerns about climate change and people's destruction of habitats? The choice is ours.

TEACH

Show the focus text. Read it aloud and invite the pupils to respond to the issues. Discuss how the text encourages us to think about the topic [e.g. the use of questions; addressing the reader directly].

Discuss the words that are highlighted. Explain that these words are possessives – they show possession. A possessive can either be a noun followed by 'apostrophe s' [e.g. the planet's future], or a possessive pronoun [e.g. ours]. We often think of 'possession' as a physical possession belonging to someone [e.g. the boy's bike], but here it is used in a wider sense. Discuss examples [e.g. 'the choice is ours' – meaning a choice we have to make; 'environmentalists' concerns' – meaning concerns raised by them].

Discuss the possessive nouns, revising the use of 'apostrophe s' [e.g. the planet's future; the world's population; the Earth's natural resources]. Recap the rules for plural possessive nouns, using examples from the focus text. For example, if the plural 'owner' already ends with 's', just add an apostrophe [environmentalists']; if the plural owner does not end with 's', add 'apostrophe s' [people's].

Discuss the use of possessive pronouns [e.g. The choice is <u>ours</u>]. Remind the pupils that there is no apostrophe in a possessive pronoun – a common mistake. Invite the pupils to replace 'ours' in this sentence with other possessive pronouns [The choice is yours/theirs/mine/his/hers].

Explain that possessive pronouns are sometimes confused with possessive *determiners* [e.g. my; our; your; their]. A determiner is always followed by a noun [e.g. our <u>choice</u>; their <u>concerns</u>], whereas a possessive pronoun stands alone in place of the noun.

EXTEND Discuss other confusions relating to possessives [e.g. its/it's].

PRACTISE

Pupil book page 39

APPLY

- Remind the pupils to check the use of possessive apostrophes when proofreading their writing, particularly where the 'possession' is not a physical item [e.g. the woman's kindness].
- The pupils write headings or sub-headings using possessive nouns [e.g. Football's fascinating facts].
- The pupils write short, dramatic sentences using possessive pronouns [e.g. The fault was hers. The decision is yours.].

ASSESS

Dictation: The doctor read the patient's notes. The patient knew the notes were <u>hers</u> because she saw her name on the front. She waited to hear the doctor's opinion about her condition.
Say: Underline the possessive pronoun.
Check: There is correct use of apostrophes with no misuse [e.g. in plurals or the possessive pronoun].

Pupil book answers

Possessives

Remember

A possessive can be a **possessive noun** (a noun followed by '**apostrophe s**') or a **possessive pronoun**. Possessive pronouns stand alone instead of a noun.

the planet's future	(possessive noun)
environmentalists' concerns	(plural possessive noun)
the choice is ours	(possessive pronoun)

Try it

1 Rewrite each phrase as a **possessive noun**. Use an **apostrophe**.

the generosity shown by the public	the public's generosity
an announcement made by the Prime Minister	the Prime Minister's announcement
impossible deeds performed by our heroes	our heroes' impossible deeds
the biography about Martin Luther King	Martin Luther King's biography
the study carried out by scientists	the scientists' study
the courage shown by the women	the women's courage

2 Rewrite each sentence using a **possessive pronoun**.

She came up with the idea.	The idea was hers.
The mistake was made by me.	The mistake was mine.
It is our responsibility.	The responsibility is ours.
You have to make the decision.	The decision is yours.
They have broken the world record.	The world record is theirs.
He gave the best performance.	The best performance was his.

Sentence practice

Write <u>three</u> sentences about opinions. Use a **possessive noun** or **possessive pronoun** in each.

This opinion is mine. Yours may be different. I always listen to other people's opinions.

39

Check that the apostrophes have been added in the correct place. Remind the pupils to check whether the noun is singular or plural.

In these phrases the idea of possession is extended beyond physical possessions belonging to a person. You may wish to discuss this with the pupils.

Check that the pupils use possessive pronouns as shown, rather than possessive determiners followed by a noun [e.g. her idea; my mistake].

Check that there is no apostrophe in the possessive pronouns.

These are just examples of possible sentences.

Check that the pupils use nouns with apostrophes or possessive pronouns, rather than possessive determiners followed by a noun [e.g. my opinion].

Check that apostrophes are used correctly in possessive nouns and not used in possessive pronouns.

Lesson 29 More relative clauses

> Focus introducing relative clauses that refer to a whole clause rather than a noun
>
> Key terms relative clause, noun, relative pronoun, main clause, subordinate clause, comma
>
> Focus text **There have been many attempts to scale Everest, <u>which is the highest mountain peak in the world</u>.**
> **In 1953, Edmund Hillary and Sherpa Tenzing were the first to reach the summit of Everest, which was a remarkable achievement with the equipment of the time.**

TEACH

Show the focus text. Read the first sentence. Discuss what two things it tells us about Everest [e.g. the information given in the main clause and in the subordinate clause]. Ask the pupils to name the underlined part of the sentence [relative clause – beginning with the relative pronoun 'which'].

Read the second sentence and discuss what information this sentence gives. Ask the pupils to identify the relative clause. Underline it [which was a remarkable achievement …].

Compare the relative clauses in the two sentences. In the first sentence, the relative clause gives more information relating to a *noun* – Everest. In the second sentence, the relative clause 'which was a remarkable achievement' refers back to the *event* of reaching the summit rather than the noun 'Everest'.

Explain that a relative clause usually tells us more about a noun, but sometimes a relative clause is attached to a whole clause, so that the relative pronoun refers back to the event expressed in that clause. This sort of relative clause is a useful way of adding a comment or something extra on to a sentence. It can avoid the use of separate sentences and the repetition of some words [e.g. in the focus text 'which was …' is used rather than repeating 'Reaching the summit was …']. Explain that relative clauses such as these are always separated from the main clause by a comma.

Invite the pupils to orally compose some other sentences, using 'which was a remarkable achievement' to refer back to an event [e.g. I scored full marks on my spelling test, which was a remarkable achievement.].

EXTEND Discuss the use of similar relative clauses in sentences with two main clauses [e.g. They were the first to reach the summit, which was a remarkable achievement, and they returned as heroes.].

PRACTISE

Pupil book page 40

APPLY

- The pupils write a chain sentence using a series of relative clauses to include several linked events [e.g. The cat jumped off the wall, which made the dog bark, which …].
- The pupils write diaries, letters or journals, using relative clauses to comment on the event[s] in a sentence [e.g. I broke a plate, which really annoyed Dad.].
- In accounts, the pupils use relative clauses to comment on events [e.g. … which was unfortunate].
- The pupils use relative clauses to explain ideas expressed in main clauses [e.g. … which means …].

ASSESS

Dictation: The washing, which had been drying on the line, was now all over the garden. We heard Mum crashing around in the kitchen, <u>which meant she was not pleased</u>.
Say: Underline the relative clause that refers to an event in the sentence.
Check: The relative clauses are correctly separated from their main clause using commas.

74

Pupil book answers

More relative clauses

Remember

Relative clauses usually give more information about a noun. However, some relative clauses refer to what is said in the whole of the **main clause**, rather than to just a noun. These relative clauses are separated from the main clause by a **comma**.

Edmund Hillary and Sherpa Tenzing were the first to reach the summit of Everest, which was a remarkable achievement.

Try it

1 Underline the **relative clause** in each sentence. Tick the box if the relative clause refers to the whole **clause**, rather than the **noun**.

There was no-one in the swimming pool, which was weird. ✓

I fed the kittens, which were only a few weeks old. ☐

In August we are going to India, which I am very excited about. ✓

Something startled the creature, which gave Beth the chance to escape. ✓

The painting, which is very old, is above the fireplace in the dining room. ☐

We chose Ethan, which was a mistake, and Evie to complete our team. ✓

> You could discuss how these relative clauses are used [e.g. to show the result of the event in the main clause; to comment on it].

2 Add a **relative clause** that refers to the **main clause**. Punctuate each sentence correctly.

We played our first league game last week , which was very exciting.

The fire is spreading through the forest , which is very worrying.

A wolf howled in the distance , which made the boy shiver.

The house is very old , which makes it an interesting place to visit.

Connor helped the man with his bags , which was very kind of him.

There was a lot of shouting in the garden , which woke the baby.

> These are just examples of relative clauses that refer back to the main clause. If the pupils have written an answer that refers to the noun [e.g. ... his bags, which were very heavy] discuss this with them.
>
> The pupils should have added a comma after the main clause and a full stop at the end of the sentence.

Sentence practice

Write <u>two</u> sentences about something bad happening. In both sentences, use a **relative clause** that refers to events in the **main clause**.

Jim fell over, which meant he hurt his leg. He couldn't play football, which really annoyed him.

40

> These are just examples of sentences using relative clauses to refer to events in the main clauses.
>
> Check that the sentences are correctly punctuated, with commas separating main and relative clauses.

Lesson 30 Conditional sentences

Focus writing conditional sentences; using modal verbs in conditional sentences

Key terms **conditional sentence**, modal verb, conjunction, main clause, subordinate clause

Focus text We should be there by ten if we leave at nine o'clock.
If the weather is fine, we will do lots of outdoor activities.
If it rains, we may need to go indoors.
The trip will go ahead unless the weather is really bad.

TEACH

Show the focus text. Explain that a teacher is discussing a future school trip with their pupils. Read the focus text and discuss the possibilities outlined by the teacher. Point out that these things are not certain; they are dependent on other things [e.g. the time they leave; the weather].

Explain that the sentences in the focus text are conditional sentences. In a conditional sentence one thing depends on another. Something will only happen *if* something else happens [e.g. they will only be there by ten if they leave at nine]. We often use conditional sentences when expressing future possibilities because things are not certain; they are often dependent on something else.

Explain that a conditional sentence has a main clause and a subordinate clause that gives a condition. The subordinate clause often begins with the conjunction 'if' and it gives the 'condition' – the thing that must happen for the event in the main clause to happen. Sometimes the conjunction 'unless' is used instead, to state the thing that will *stop* the event happening [e.g. unless it rains].

Underline the [conditional] subordinate clauses in the focus text [if we leave at nine o'clock; If the weather is fine; If it rains; unless the weather is really bad] to show that they can be placed first or second in the sentence. If the subordinate clause is at the start of a sentence, it is followed by a comma. Orally reorder the clauses in the focus text to show that this does not affect the sentence's meaning.

Circle the modal verbs in the main clauses [should, will, may]. Explain that modal verbs are used in conditional sentences to show different levels of possibility. Discuss which outcomes seem most certain [e.g. ... we will do lots of outdoor activities] and which less certain [e.g. ... we may need to go indoors].

EXTEND Discuss the use of conditional sentences to express ideas about the past [e.g. how things would/might have been different – 'If I had known it was going to rain, I would [not] have ...'].

PRACTISE

Pupil book page 41

APPLY

- The pupils use conditional sentences to make predictions about a story, exploring future possibilities [e.g. If Andrew finds him, he might/will/could ...].
- In other areas of the curriculum, the pupils use conditional sentences to make predictions or talk about future possibilities [e.g. If I let go of the weight, it might/will ...].
- In factual writing, the pupils use conditionals to express ideas about the past and the future.
- The pupils use 'what if' ideas in poems or imaginative writing [e.g. If I could change the world ...].

ASSESS

Dictation: If you make the school holidays longer, children could take part in more sports.
Say: Write another sentence starting with the same subordinate clause.
Answer: e.g. If you make the school holidays longer, we will be very happy.

Pupil book answers

Conditional sentences

Remember

A **conditional sentence** is a sentence in which one thing depends on another. It has a **main clause** and a **subordinate clause**. The subordinate clause starts with a **conjunction** such as 'if' or 'unless', and states the 'condition' needed for the event in the main clause to happen.

We should be there by ten if we leave at nine o'clock.

If the weather is fine, we will do lots of outdoor activities.

The trip will go ahead unless the weather is really bad.

Try it

1 Underline the **subordinate clause** that gives the condition in each sentence.

If the weather improves, we could visit the coast this weekend.

I won't set the people free unless you promise to help me.

If we can persuade someone famous to open our summer fair, lots of people will come.

My little brother won't go swimming unless I go with him.

If you listen to a lot of loud music, it can damage your ears.

Our planet will not survive unless we take care of it.

2 Rewrite each sentence, adding a **subordinate clause** that gives a condition.

Superman will save the planet.

If he defeats his enemy, Superman will save the planet.

I can raise a lot of money for this important charity.

If you sponsor me, I can raise a lot of money for this important charity.

The crops will fail and people will starve.

The crops will fail and people will starve unless it rains soon.

Sentence practice

You are going to the beach at the weekend. Write <u>three</u> **conditional** sentences about what you might do.

If it is warm, I will swim in the sea. If it is cold, we might go for a walk to keep warm. We could hire a boat unless it is too expensive.

These are just examples. The conditional subordinate clause can be added at the start or end of the sentence. If it is at the start of the sentence, it should be followed by a comma.

You could discuss other conjunctions that can be used in conditional sentences [e.g. As long as ...].

41

These are just examples of sentences with conditional subordinate clauses suggesting possibilities. Look for subordinate clauses at the start or end of the sentences. Subordinate clauses at the start of a sentence should be followed by a comma.

The pupils could use 'unless' [or 'as long as'] rather than 'if' [e.g. unless it rains; as long as it is warm].

Revision 3 answers

These pages revise terms and concepts introduced in **Grammar 4** and earlier in this book. The focus of each activity is given to help identify areas that may need further reinforcement.

Grammar 5 · Schofield & Sims **Grammar and Punctuation**

Revision 3

Focus: identifying pronouns

Remind the pupils that pronouns stand in place of nouns [e.g. 'it' = the game].

1 Underline all the **pronouns** in the sentence.

Dad said <u>I</u> should save up and buy the game <u>myself</u> if <u>I</u> want <u>it</u> so badly.

2 Underline the **pronoun** in each sentence and write the **nouns** they refer to.

All birds have wings, although <u>some</u> cannot fly.   birds

All birds have beaks and <u>they</u> use <u>these</u> to find food.   birds   beaks

Many children love sweets and <u>they</u> often buy <u>them</u>.   children   sweets

Amy has lost her pen. Tell <u>her</u> if you see <u>it</u>.   Amy   pen

Sean has a new green jacket. <u>It</u> really suits <u>him</u>.   jacket   Sean

3 Rewrite each sentence using the **past perfect verb form** rather than the simple past tense.

The pond froze overnight.   The pond had frozen overnight.

The ship sank in the storm.   The ship had sunk in the storm.

I wrote to the council.   I had written to the council.

She tore the paper in half.   She had torn the paper in half.

4 Rewrite each sentence, changing it from indirect speech to **direct speech**.

Amina said my dancing was absolutely amazing.

"Your dancing is absolutely amazing," said Amina.

Imran asked if I had found the secret key.

"Have you found the secret key?" asked Imran.

5 Insert the missing **punctuation** in these examples of **direct speech**.

"You will be safe here," said the young girl, "until the morning."

The doctor said, "I think you should stay home from school today."

"I have made you many gifts," said the cunning goldsmith. "Edwin will show them to you."

"It's lovely and sunny outside," said Dad. "I'm going for a walk by the river."

Focus: identifying pronouns

Remind the pupils that pronouns stand in place of nouns [e.g. 'it' = the game].

Focus: pronouns for cohesion

Focus: past perfect form of verbs

Remind the pupils that the past perfect form uses the auxiliary/'helper' verb 'had' alongside the main verb. These sentences feature verbs with irregular past perfect forms, so check that the pupils have made the necessary changes to the main verb [e.g. 'had sunk', not 'had sank'].

Focus: inverted commas and other punctuation to indicate direct speech

Check that the pupils have also reworded the indirect speech as direct speech without significantly changing the meaning.

Focus: inverted commas and other punctuation to indicate direct speech

All punctuation should be correct.

The first two examples should be punctuated as one sentence. The last example should be punctuated as two sentences.

6 Underline all the **determiners** in the sentences below.

There is <u>one</u> banana and <u>some</u> grapes left in <u>the</u> fruit bowl but <u>no</u> apples.

<u>Your</u> friend has <u>two</u> sisters, I have <u>three</u> brothers and you have <u>a</u> twin.

Can you see <u>the</u> difference between <u>this</u> picture and <u>that</u> picture?

7 Add a different **determiner** to each **noun**.

_____an_____	actor	_____some_____	fabric	_____two_____	desks
_____this_____	music	_____my_____	computer	_____these_____	geese
_____the_____	traffic	_____many_____	factories	_____his_____	hair

8 Make each **noun** into an expanded **noun phrase** by adding a **determiner**, **adjectives** and a **prepositional phrase**.

lizard   the fearsome-looking lizard with eyes on stalks

sword   his legendary sword of burnished gold

stadium   this modern stadium with luxurious seating

corridor   an empty corridor on an abandoned space station

9 Use the **pronouns** 'I' and 'me' to correctly complete the sentences below.

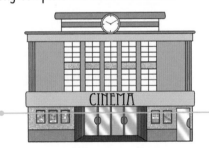

Greg told Belle and _____me_____ where he was going.

Katie and _____I_____ are going to the cinema after school.

Mum made cheese-and-pickle sandwiches for Ben and _____me_____ .

I think Prashin and _____I_____ might make a model castle.

10 Complete each sentence using a different **modal verb**.

The kite _____might_____ blow away in this wind.

We _____could_____ go to the coffee shop later.

I _____will_____ need a rest soon.

You _____may_____ get a mountain bike for your birthday.

You _____should_____ not stay up too late.

43

Focus: identifying determiners

Remind the pupils that a determiner comes before a noun or noun phrase.

Focus: determiners

These are just examples of possible determiners. The pupils should not have used 'a'/'an' or 'the' more than once. Plural nouns will need a 'plural determiner' [e.g. two/some/many desks].

Focus: expanded noun phrases

These are just examples of possible expanded noun phrases with determiners, adjectives and prepositional phrases. Compare the pupils' answers, discussing how they give detail about the noun.

Focus: Standard English pronouns

If necessary, remind the pupils that we use 'I' if it is the subject of the sentence [i.e. before the verb], and 'me' if it is after the verb.

Focus: modal verbs

The pupils could use other modal verbs in the sentences. You could discuss how the choice of modal verb affects the meaning of the sentence, showing certainty [e.g. will] or possibility [e.g. might].

Writing task 3: Analysis sheet

Tick the circles to show amount of evidence found in writing:
1 No evidence
2 Some evidence
3 Clear evidence

Pupil name: _____

Date: _____

Assessing punctuation

The writing sample demonstrates:	Evidence		
sentence boundaries demarcated with capital letters and appropriate end punctuation, with capital letters also used for 'I' and proper nouns.	①	②	③
commas correctly used in lists to separate words, phrases and clauses, as well as after fronted adverbials and before question tags.	①	②	③
apostrophes used correctly in contractions and for possession.	①	②	③
direct speech puncuated correctly, including when spoken words are split.	①	②	③
the use of punctuation to indicate parenthesis [commas, brackets or dashes].	①	②	③

Assessing grammar and sentence structure

The writing sample demonstrates:	Evidence		
grammatically correct sentences that show variation and use Standard English [e.g. correct subject–verb agreement].	①	②	③
expanded noun phrases to convey information concisely [e.g. an important habitat for wildlife].	①	②	③
adverbials to add detail and indicate viewpoint [e.g. hopefully; sadly].	①	②	③
subordinate clauses, including a range of conjunctions to link and develop ideas.	①	②	③
pronouns to avoid repetition and aid cohesion.	①	②	③
varied use of verb forms to show time references, including perfect forms [e.g. it has been here …].	①	②	③
relative clauses, to clarify and develop ideas [e.g. The tower, which is an important local landmark, …].	①	②	③
modal verbs and adverbs to express possibility or future events [e.g. there might; it would/could].	①	②	③
conditional sentences to express future possibilities [e.g. If the library closes, children will have to buy all the books they want to read].	①	②	③

Key target: _____

Writing task 3: Pupil checklist

Name: _____ Date: _____

Reread what you have written to check that it makes sense. Tick the circle if you have correctly used the punctuation or grammar feature in your writing.

Punctuation

◯ I have used capital letters at the beginning of sentences, and full stops, question marks or exclamation marks at the end of sentences.

◯ I have used capital letters for 'I' and proper nouns.

◯ I have used commas in lists and to separate words, phrases and clauses.

◯ I have used apostrophes in contractions and for possession.

◯ I have used inverted commas and other punctuation in direct speech.

◯ I have used punctuation to indicate parenthesis (commas, brackets or dashes).

Grammar and sentences

◯ I have used grammatically correct sentences and Standard English.

◯ I have used different types of sentence and different sentence openings.

◯ I have used expanded noun phrases to describe and give details.

◯ I have used adverbials to add detail and show viewpoint.

◯ I have used sentences with subordinate clauses and a range of conjunctions.

◯ I have used pronouns and it is clear who or what they refer to.

◯ I have used different verb forms including progressive and perfect forms.

◯ I have used relative clauses to clarify or develop ideas.

◯ I have used modal verbs to suggest possibilities or future events.

◯ I have used conditional sentences to express future possibilities.

Teacher feedback

My key target: _____

_____

Final test

Name: _____

1 Write the underlined words as **contractions**.

<u>You had</u> better hurry or <u>they will</u> go without you.

_____   _____

1 mark

2 Underline all the words in the sentence that need a **capital letter**.

pupils at marchmead primary school in leeds have been learning chinese since september.

1 mark

3 Add a **prefix** to each verb to make new words.

_____power   _____qualify

_____awaken   _____inform

_____hydrate   _____sleep

1 mark

4 Underline the **past progressive** verb form in the passage below.

Jason walked down Faraday Street. It was late now and all the shop owners were packing up for the weekend. Mr Jones had closed his shop already. All the lights were switched off and the shutters had been pulled down.

1 mark

5 Underline the **relative pronoun** in the sentence below.

Some gases damage the ozone layer that protects us from the sun.

1 mark

6 Rewrite this **command** using an **adverbial** at the start of the sentence. Punctuate your sentence correctly.

Send me a postcard.

_____

1 mark

7 Underline the **subordinate clause** in each sentence.

He was able to disappear whenever he wanted to.

Immediately after lunch, we went for a walk even though it was raining.

As soon as the show ended, everyone stood up and began to clap.

1 mark

8 Look at where the arrow is pointing. Which **punctuation mark** is missing?

"Don't run away," Meena shouted desperately ↑ "Noah, tell them to stop."

comma ☐   exclamation mark ☐

full stop ☐   question mark ☐

1 mark

9 Underline the **relative clause** in the sentence below.

The people who have moved in next door seem very friendly.

1 mark

10 Write a sentence using a **verb** formed from the word 'drama'.

_____

1 mark

11 Complete the sentence below so that it uses the **present perfect** form of a verb.

I _____ lots of photographs.

1 mark

12 Tick <u>one</u> box in each row to show how the **modal verb** affects the meaning of the sentence.

Sentence	Modal verb shows certainty	Modal verb shows possibility
I will do my homework.		
Jess might find her bag.		
Ed can ride a horse.		
We could go to the concert.		

1 mark

13 Rewrite the sentence below so that it is written in **Standard English**.

I haven't heard nothing. _____

1 mark

14 Underline the part of the sentence that should be in **brackets**.

The house built nearly two hundred years ago will soon be open to the public.

1 mark

15 Choose the correct word from the brackets to complete the sentences using **Standard English**.

Shall I take _____ books back to the library?   (them those)

There's the dog _____ I saw in the playground.   (that what)

I have lost _____ gloves and _____ hands are cold.   (me my)

1 mark

16 Tick <u>all</u> the sentences that include a **preposition**.

In winter, life can be hard for some animals. ☐

Food is hard to find because of the cold. ☐

Some animals hibernate during the winter. ☐

They store food away before they go to sleep. ☐

☐
1 mark

17 Insert <u>two</u> **commas** in the correct place in the sentence below.

Stephanie Carter the owner of the business was delighted to receive the award.

☐
1 mark

18 Rewrite the sentence below adding an **adverb** to make the event sound less certain.

I could be there by six o'clock. _____

☐
1 mark

19 Explain how the use of **commas** changes the meaning of these two sentences.

Daisy the dog is digging up the garden.

Daisy, the dog is digging up the garden.

_____

_____

☐
1 mark

20 Rewrite this sentence using **dashes** to punctuate the **parenthesis**.

He didn't see us no-one did, surprisingly as we climbed out of the window.

_____

☐
1 mark

End of test

Final test: Mark scheme

Q	Focus	Answer
1	apostrophes to mark contractions	**Award 1 mark** for <u>both</u> correct contractions. You'd they'll Correct spelling and correct placement of the apostrophe are required. 'You'd' should begin with a capital letter as it is at the start of a sentence.
2	capital letters for names of people, places, days of the week	**Award 1 mark** for all <u>seven</u> words correctly underlined. <u>pupils</u> at <u>marchmead</u> <u>primary</u> <u>school</u> in <u>leeds</u> have been learning <u>chinese</u> since <u>september</u>.
3	verb prefixes [e.g. dis–, de–, mis–, over–, re–]	**Award 1 mark** for <u>six</u> correctly spelt verbs. over/re/depower disqualify reawaken misinform de/rehydrate oversleep
4	identifying progressive verb forms	**Award 1 mark** for the correct verb form underlined. were packing
5	identifying relative pronouns	**Award 1 mark** for the correct word underlined. Some gases damage the ozone layer <u>that</u> protects us from the sun.
6	fronted adverbials: commands with fronted adverbials	**Award 1 mark** for a grammatically correct sentence with a comma after the fronted adverbial, e.g. When you have a minute, send me a postcard. Before you leave, send me a postcard. In the morning, send me a postcard.
7	subordinate clauses: using a wide range of conjunctions	**Award 1 mark** for all <u>three</u> subordinate clauses correctly identified. He was able to disappear <u>whenever he wanted to</u>. Immediately after lunch, we went for a walk <u>even though it was raining</u>. <u>As soon as the show ended</u>, everyone stood up and began to clap.
8	full stops to demarcate sentences	**Award 1 mark** for the correct box ticked. full stop ✓
9	identifying relative clauses	**Award 1 mark** for the correct part of the sentence underlined. The people <u>who have moved in next door</u> seem very friendly.
10	converting nouns or adjectives into verbs using suffixes [e.g. –ate, –ise, –ify]	**Award 1 mark** for any grammatically correct sentence that uses the verb 'dramatise', e.g. We are going to <u>dramatise</u> the story about Theseus. The spelling 'dramatize' is also acceptable. *Do not accept* sentences using the word 'dramatic', as this is an adjective. The sentence should also be correctly punctuated.
11	verbs in the perfect form	**Award 1 mark** for a verb in the present perfect form that makes sense in the sentence, e.g. have taken/have found

| 12 | modal verbs indicating degrees of possibility | **Award 1 mark** for a correctly completed table. |

Sentence	Certainty	Possibility
I will do my homework.	✓	
Jess might find her bag.		✓
Ed can ride a horse.	✓	
We could go to the concert.		✓

13	Standard English: double negatives	**Award 1 mark** for a correctly punctuated sentence that avoids the double negative, e.g. I haven't heard anything. I've heard nothing.
14	punctuation for parenthesis	**Award 1 mark** for the parenthesis underlined. The house <u>built nearly two hundred years ago</u> will soon be open to the public.
15	Standard English pronouns	**Award 1 mark** for the <u>four</u> words correctly identified. Shall I take <u>those</u> books back to the library? There's the dog <u>that</u> I saw in the playground. I have lost <u>my</u> gloves and <u>my</u> hands are cold.
16	prepositions expressing time, place and cause	**Award 1 mark** for all <u>three</u> correct sentences ticked. In winter, life can be hard for some animals. ✓ Food is hard to find because of the cold. ✓ Some animals hibernate during the winter. ✓
17	commas to indicate parenthesis	**Award 1 mark** for <u>both</u> correctly placed commas. Stephanie Carter, the owner of the business, was delighted to receive the award.
18	adverbs indicating degrees of possibility	**Award 1 mark** for a correctly punctuated sentence using an adverb to show that it is possible but not certain, e.g. <u>Perhaps</u>, I could be there by six o'clock. I could <u>possibly</u> be there by six o'clock.
19	commas to clarify meaning	**Award 1 mark** for an explanation of the meaning of <u>both</u> sentences, e.g. Without the comma it means a dog called Daisy is digging up the garden. With the comma it means Daisy is being told that the dog is digging up the garden.
20	dashes to indicate parenthesis	**Award 1 mark** for a correctly punctuated sentence using <u>two</u> dashes. He didn't see us – no-one did, surprisingly – as we climbed out of the window.

Final test: Analysis sheet

Tick the box for each correct answer.

Q	Focus	Pupil names									
1	apostrophes to mark contractions										
2	capital letters for names of people, places, days of the week										
3	verb prefixes [e.g. dis–, de–, mis–, over–, re–]										
4	identifying progressive verb forms										
5	identifying relative pronouns										
6	fronted adverbials: commands with fronted adverbials										
7	subordinate clauses: using a wide range of conjunctions										
8	full stops to demarcate sentences										
9	identifying relative clauses										
10	converting nouns or adjectives into verbs using suffixes [e.g. –ate, –ise, –ify]										
11	verbs in the perfect form										
12	modal verbs indicating degrees of possibility										
13	Standard English: double negatives										
14	punctuation for parenthesis										
15	Standard English pronouns										
16	prepositions expressing time, place and cause										
17	commas to indicate parenthesis										
18	adverbs indicating degrees of possibility										
19	commas to clarify meaning										
20	dashes to indicate parenthesis										
Total correct answers per pupil											

Target tracking sheet

Group: _____

Target: _____

Date set: _____   Date for review: _____

Tick the circles to show depth of understanding:
1 Just beginning
2 Progressing
3 Learning is embedded

Pupil name	Evidence from independent writing	Progress in independent writing		
		①	②	③
		①	②	③
		①	②	③
		①	②	③
		①	②	③
		①	②	③
		①	②	③
		①	②	③
		①	②	③
		①	②	③

Learning pathways sheet

Pupil name: _____

Date last updated: _____

Tick the circles to show depth of understanding:
1 Just beginning
2 Progressing
3 Learning is embedded

Punctuation pathway

Demarcate sentences with capital letters, full stops, question marks and exclamation marks.
1   2   3

Use capital letters for 'I' and proper nouns.
1   2   3

Use commas to separate items in a list.
1   2   3

Use apostrophes for singular and plural possession and in contractions.
1   2   3

Use inverted commas and other punctuation to indicate direct speech.
1   2   3

Use commas to separate phrases and clauses and avoid ambiguity.
1   2   3

Use brackets, commas or dashes to mark parenthesis.
1   2   3

Grammar and sentence pathway

Write grammatically correct sentences that show variation and use Standard English.
1   2   3

Use tense accurately, including progressive and perfect forms.
1   2   3

Use co-ordinating and subordinating conjunctions to write sentences with more than one clause.
1   2   3

Use expanded noun phrases to add detail.
1   2   3

Use adverbials to add detail, make links and vary sentence openings.
1   2   3

Use pronouns to avoid repetition.
1   2   3

Use relative clauses to clarify and explain.
1   2   3

Glossary

Adjective
An **adjective** is a word used to modify or specify a noun [e.g. an <u>angry</u> man; the <u>red</u> car]. Lesson 12
- **Comparative** and **superlative adjectives** are used to compare nouns. The suffixes –er and –est are added to shorter adjectives [e.g. the faster car; the fastest car]. The words 'more' and 'most' are used with longer adjectives [e.g. a more expensive car; the most expensive car].
- Some adjectives are formed by adding a suffix to a word [e.g. care<u>ful</u>; care<u>less</u>].
- Some adjectives are formed by adding both a suffix and a prefix [e.g. <u>un</u>remark<u>able</u>].

Adverb
An **adverb** is a word that modifies a verb or action in a sentence. An adverb can specify *how*, *where*, or *when* the action took place [e.g. He arrived <u>quietly</u>. He arrived <u>outside</u>. He arrived <u>yesterday</u>.]. Sometimes adverbs modify other words, such as another adverb [e.g. <u>really</u> quickly] or an adjective [e.g. a <u>really</u> good idea]. Lessons 1 and 25
- Some adverbs [and **adverbials**] are used to show links between ideas or events [e.g. 'meanwhile' shows a time link; 'therefore' shows the result of an action; 'firstly'/'secondly' show a number of points]. They help link sentences and paragraphs and achieve text cohesion. Lessons 23 and 24
- Some adverbs are used to show how likely or possible an event is [e.g. 'surely' – very likely; 'perhaps' – a possibility]. Lesson 17
- Some adverbs comment on the whole sentence or clause [e.g. <u>Fortunately</u>, the rain stopped.]. Lesson 26

Adverbial
An **adverbial** is a word, phrase or clause that is used like an adverb – it adds more detail about a verb or event in a sentence. Adverbs can be used as adverbials, as can phrases, including prepositional phrases [e.g. He arrived <u>in the morning</u>. He arrived <u>at the gate</u>. He arrived <u>in a hurry</u>.] or noun phrases [e.g. He arrived <u>last night</u>.]. Lesson 1 Subordinate clauses starting with conjunctions can also be adverbials [e.g. He arrived <u>after I left</u>.]. Lessons 1 and 2
- **Fronted adverbials** are adverbial words, phrases or clauses used at the start of a sentence [e.g. <u>Suddenly</u>, the ghost appeared. <u>In the morning</u>, I lay in bed. <u>Although the sun was rising</u>, he slept on.]. Commas are always used after fronted adverbials to separate them from the rest of the sentence. Lessons 1 and 2

Ambiguity
Ambiguity occurs when there is more than one possible meaning, for example when it is not clear who or what a pronoun refers to [e.g. He dropped the computer on his leg and it broke.]. Lesson 6
- Sometimes punctuation is needed to help avoid ambiguity. For example, commas can help to clarify the meaning of a sentence [e.g. 'Keep tackling, Joe.' rather than 'Keep tackling Joe.']. Lesson 22

Apostrophe
An **apostrophe** ['] is a punctuation mark with two different uses:
- it shows the position of missing letters in **contractions**, or shortened forms of words that are often used in informal speech [e.g. can't; who's; we've].
- it is used with the letter 's' in the **possessive** form of nouns [e.g. Sam's hat; both boys' coats; the children's shoes]. Lesson 28

Clause

A **clause** is a group of words that are connected together and include a verb. A clause can be a complete sentence or part of a sentence.

- A **main clause** is a clause that makes sense independently and so could be a sentence in itself [e.g. He paused.]. A sentence always contains at least one main clause, and can contain more than one if the clauses are linked with a co-ordinating conjunction [e.g. He paused <u>and</u> then he spoke.].
- A **subordinate clause** is a less important clause that is added to a main clause, for example by using a subordinating conjunction. It adds extra detail [e.g. He paused <u>before he spoke</u>.]. The subordinate clause 'before he spoke' does not make sense without the main clause. Lesson 2
- A **relative clause** is a type of subordinate clause. It usually adds more detail about the noun, although it can comment on a whole clause. Relative clauses begin with a relative pronoun, which refers back to someone or something already mentioned [e.g. There was a king <u>**who** had nothing</u>. He wore a crown <u>**that** was made of tin</u>.]. Sometimes the relative pronoun is omitted [e.g. The King wore a crown made of tin.]. Lessons 13, 14 and 29

Cohesion

A text has **cohesion** when it is clear how the ideas in the sentences and paragraphs link together. Linking adverbials, pronouns and the use of repeated words and phrases can all help to achieve cohesion in a text. Lessons 23 and 24

Comma

A **comma [,]** is a punctuation mark used to separate different parts of a sentence, for example:

- to separate the items in a list [e.g. She put the fresh eggs, a packet of cheese and some butter in the basket.].
- to separate spoken words from non-spoken words in direct speech [e.g. "I'm hungry," he said.]. Lessons 3 and 21
- to separate a fronted adverbial from the rest of the sentence [e.g. In the forest, the wolf was waiting.]. Lessons 1, 2 and 21
- to indicate a parenthesis in a sentence [e.g. Jamie's mother, who was a great cook, had been baking all day.]. Lesson 16
- to avoid ambiguity and make the meaning of a sentence clear [e.g. Keep tackling, Joe.]. Lesson 22

Conditional sentence

In a **conditional sentence**, one thing depends on another. A conditional sentence has a main clause and a subordinate clause that gives a condition. The subordinate clause often begins with the conjunction 'if' and gives the condition. Sometimes the conjunction 'unless' is used. Lesson 30

Conjunction

A **conjunction** is a word that joins two words, phrases or clauses together. Conjunctions show how ideas link together [e.g. 'because' shows cause; 'when', 'while' and 'until' show time links; 'but' and 'although' show contrast].

There are two types of conjunction:

- **Co-ordinating conjunctions** [and, but, or] link together two words, phrases or clauses that are equally important [e.g. Bill <u>and</u> Diane were looking for a house <u>or</u> a flat. Bill preferred a house <u>but</u> Diane wanted a flat.].
- **Subordinating conjunctions** [e.g. because; when; while] introduce a subordinate or less important clause [e.g. Bill preferred to live in a house <u>because</u> he wanted a garden.]. Lesson 2

Determiner

A **determiner** is the word that is used before a noun [e.g. a cat; this dog]. In a noun phrase, the determiner comes before any adjectives [e.g. a little cat; this big dog]. It helps to specify the noun as known [e.g. my school; this school] or unknown [e.g. a school; some schools]. Lesson 11

- **Articles** ['the', 'a' and 'an'] are the most common determiners. 'The' is the definite article. It shows that the noun that it precedes is known [e.g. 'the dog']. 'A' or 'an' are indefinite articles. They show that the noun that they precede is unknown [e.g. a cat; an elephant]. 'An' is used before a word beginning with a vowel sound.
- Many other words can also be used as determiners, including demonstratives [e.g. this school], possessives [e.g. your school] and quantifiers [e.g. some schools]. Some of these words can also be used in other ways, for example as pronouns, but they are determiners when they are followed by a noun or noun phrase. Lesson 27

Direct and indirect speech

Direct speech records what someone says using the speaker's original words. **Indirect speech** reports what was said but does not use the exact words of the speaker. Lessons 3 and 4

- **Inverted commas**, sometimes called **speech marks**, are used to mark the beginning and end of the spoken words in direct speech [e.g. "My name is Jack."]. Direct speech is often followed by a reporting clause [unspoken words that say who is speaking]. A comma is placed within the inverted commas at the end of the spoken words [e.g. "My name is Jack," said the boy.]. If the spoken words are a question or an exclamation, then a question mark or exclamation mark is used instead of the comma [e.g. "What is your name?" asked the boy.]. Lesson 3
- If the unspoken words come first, a comma is used to separate the unspoken words from the spoken words [e.g. Maya said, "Listen to that."]. If the unspoken words are placed in the middle of a spoken sentence, two commas are needed [e.g. "I heard it before," said Maya, "but this time it's louder."]. Lessons 3 and 4

Noun

Nouns are words that name things, people and places [e.g. car; man]. These are **common nouns**.

- **Proper nouns** are the names of specific people, places and things [e.g. Joe Henson; Banbury Park; February]. Proper nouns start with a capital letter.
- A **compound noun** is a noun made up of two root words joined together [e.g. footpath; butterfly].
- An **abstract noun** is a noun that does not describe a person, place or thing but rather names an idea or quality [e.g. bravery]. These words are often formed by adding suffixes such as –ness to adjectives.
- A **collective noun** refers to a whole group of things [e.g. a class of children].
- A **noun phrase** is a group of words built around a noun. An expanded noun phrase might include a determiner, adjective[s], nouns and/or prepositional phrases [e.g. the fast police car with flashing lights]. Lesson 12

Paragraph

A **paragraph** is a group of sentences that go together because they have one main idea or theme. Paragraphs are used to organise ideas in writing. Lessons 23 and 24

Parenthesis

A **parenthesis** is a word, phrase or clause that is inserted into a sentence to add extra information. **Brackets, dashes** or **commas** are used to separate the parenthesis from the rest of the sentence [e.g. Jamie Brown (my best friend) is a talented football player.]. Lessons 15 and 16

Phrase

A **phrase** is a group of words that are connected together.
- A **noun phrase** is a group of words built around a noun. An expanded noun phrase might include a determiner, adjective[s], nouns and/or prepositional phrases [e.g. the fast police car with flashing lights]. Lesson 12
- A **prepositional phrase** is a group of words starting with a preposition [e.g. in the morning; under the bridge].

Prefix

A **prefix** is a group of letters added to the start of an existing word to make another word. Adding a prefix changes the meaning of the original word, for example changing the meaning of adjectives or verbs [e.g. unpleasant, dishonest; undo, reconnect, overload]. Lesson 20
- Some prefixes create negative meanings [e.g. unwelcome; disagree].
- Other prefixes have specific meanings [e.g. replay – 're' means 'again'; submarine – 'sub' means 'under'].

Preposition

A **preposition** is a word that shows how one thing relates to another in terms of place [e.g. in the bin; behind the tree; from the window], time [e.g. before dinner; during dinner; after dinner] or cause [e.g. due to the weather].
- A preposition is always followed by a noun, pronoun or noun phrase and this creates a **prepositional phrase** [e.g. before breakfast; before him; before the storm].
- Some words, such as 'before', can act as prepositions or conjunctions. They are prepositions if they are followed by a noun, pronoun or noun phrase. They are conjunctions if followed by a clause. Lesson 27

Pronoun

A **pronoun** is a word that stands in place of a noun, proper noun or noun phrase. We use them to avoid repetition and improve cohesion. Lessons 5, 6 and 24
- **Personal pronouns** are the most commonly used pronouns [e.g. he/him; they/them]. Lesson 5
- **Possessive pronouns** are used to show possession [e.g. This pencil is mine.]. Lessons 5 and 28
- **Relative pronouns** [who, whose, which, that] are used at the start of relative clauses. Lesson 13
- **Reflexive pronouns** are used to refer back to the subject [e.g. myself; himself]. Lesson 5
- **Indefinite pronouns** are used when the noun is unknown [e.g. someone]. Lesson 5
- Other words, such as **determiners**, can be used as pronouns when they stand in place of a noun [e.g. This is mine.]. Lessons 5 and 27

Overuse of pronouns can lead to ambiguity about who or what the pronoun refers to. Lesson 6

Sentence

A **sentence** is a group of words put together to say something that makes sense. A sentence starts with a capital letter and ends with a full stop [.], question mark [?] or exclamation mark [!]. A sentence may consist of one clause or more than one clause. Sentences can be made longer by adding words, phrases and clauses that give more detail.

There are different forms of sentence with different functions and different grammatical patterns.

- **Statements** give information. They usually start with a subject followed by a verb [e.g. Joe ran away.].
- **Questions** ask for information and need a response. They can be formed using a question word [e.g. <u>What</u> is the weather like today?], a subject–verb reversal [e.g. <u>Is it</u> cold today?] or a question tag [e.g. It is cold today, <u>isn't it?</u>]. Questions always end with a question mark.
- **Commands** direct someone to do something. The main clause starts with a verb [e.g. Come here.].
- **Exclamations** express strong emotions and always end with an exclamation mark. A strict definition of an exclamation refers to sentences starting with 'What' or 'How' [e.g. What a surprise! How amazing!]. However, **interjections** are also exclamatory [e.g. Oh dear!].
- Exclamation marks are sometimes added to other sentences to make exclamatory statements [e.g. It was great!] or exclamatory commands [e.g. Stop right there!]. However, this does not change the form of the sentence.

A positive sentence can be made into a negative one by using negative words [e.g. no; not; never]. However, it is important to avoid using two negative words together, as 'double negatives' create ambiguity. Lesson 10

Sentence punctuation

Sentence punctuation refers to the use of capital letters and full stops to show the boundaries between sentences. It is an important part of punctuation as it helps to make the meaning of a text clear.

- A **question mark [?]** is used in place of a full stop if a sentence is a question.
- An **exclamation mark [!]** is used for exclamations or to show strong feeling.
- **Capital letters** are also used at the start of names and for the word 'I'.

Singular and plural

Many nouns have **singular** and **plural** forms. Singular means just one; plural means more than one. Many plurals are formed by adding –s or –es to the singular noun [e.g. cat<u>s</u>; dog<u>s</u>; fox<u>es</u>; lad<u>ies</u>]. However, some nouns have irregular plural forms [e.g. child – children; mouse – mice]. Some nouns are the same in the plural as they are in the singular [e.g. sheep; fish], and some nouns are always plural [e.g. scissors]. Non-countable nouns do not have a plural form [e.g. butter].

Standard English

Standard English is the form of English usually used in writing or formal speech. Non-Standard English is sometimes used in informal or local speech. Non-Standard English is sometimes shown in the use of verb forms [e.g. 'I done it.' rather than 'I did it.'; 'We was late.' rather than 'We were late.'], pronouns [e.g. 'me brother and me went' rather than 'my brother and I went'] and adverbs ['e.g. 'He ran quick.' rather than 'He ran quickly.']. Other examples of non-Standard forms include double negatives. Lessons 9, 10 and 25

Suffix

A **suffix** is a group of letters added to the end of an existing word to make another word. Suffixes often change words into different word classes [e.g. forming adjectives – 'wonder<u>ful</u>', 'power<u>less</u>', 'fam<u>ous</u>'; nouns – 'kind<u>ness</u>', 'entertain<u>ment</u>'; or verbs – 'solid<u>ify</u>']. Lesson 19

Verb

A **verb** is a 'doing' or 'being' word [e.g. He <u>ran</u>. He <u>is</u> sad.]. Verbs are important because they tell us about the actions in the sentence.

- Verbs also show **tense**. The tense tells us *when* the action happened – in the past or present. Many past-tense verbs are formed by adding –ed [e.g. waited; stopped; hurried]. Some verbs have irregular past-tense forms [e.g. see/saw; forget/forgot].
- Sometimes additional verbs, called **auxiliary verbs**, are used in a sentence alongside the main verb. These are 'helper' verbs [e.g. <u>has</u> come; <u>is</u> going]. Lesson 7
- **Progressive forms** [also called continuous forms] can be used in the present and past tense to describe events that are, or were, in progress for some time. They use the –ing form of the verb with the helper [or auxiliary] verb 'am/are/is' in the present tense or 'was/were' in the past tense [e.g. He <u>is</u> sin<u>ging</u>. She <u>was</u> wal<u>king</u>.]. Lesson 7
- **Perfect form**s are used to show time-and-cause relationships. The **present perfect form** of a verb is used to refer to events in the past, particularly when an event that began in the past is ongoing or still has consequences now [e.g. The tent <u>has started</u> to leak.]. It is formed using the helper [or auxiliary] verb 'has/have'. The **past perfect form**, formed using 'had', is used to refer back to an event that took place earlier [e.g. He <u>had arrived</u> before we got there.]. Lessons 7 and 8
- **Modal verbs** are auxiliary verbs that modify the meaning of other verbs, for example in order to show possibility or certainty [e.g. <u>might</u> come; <u>must</u> come]. Lesson 18
- **Conditional sentences** are used to describe events that are dependent on other events [e.g. I will be sad <u>if you move away</u>.]. Lesson 30

Word class

Every word belongs to a **word class**. The word class shows how the word is used. The main word classes are noun, verb, adjective, adverb, pronoun, conjunction, preposition and determiner. Lesson 27

- **Homonyms** are words that sound the same and are spelt the same but have different meanings. This means they can belong in different word classes. The context in which a word is used in a particular sentence determines its meaning and which word class it belongs to [e.g. He did <u>well</u>. He fetched water from the <u>well</u>.]. Lesson 27

Word family

Words in the same **word family** are related by meaning and how they are formed. They share the same **root word** [e.g. family, familiar] or a common root [e.g. horror, horrible].

- A root word is a stand-alone word without any prefixes or suffixes added to it [e.g. 'build' is the root word of 'builder', 'rebuild', 'building'].